INTRODUCING
DANCE
in Christian
Worship

Ronald Gagne
Thomas Kane
Robert VerEecke

with Introduction
by Carla DeSola

and Annotated
Bibliography
by Gloria Weyman

The Pastoral Press Washington, D.C.

Printed in the United States of America.

THE PASTORAL PRESS
225 Sheridan Street NW
Washington, DC 20011

The Pastoral Press is the book
publishing division of The National
Association of Pastoral Musicians
a membership organization of
musicians and clergy dedicated to
fostering the art of musical liturgy.

Preparation and production of
*Introducing Dance in Christian
Worship* was supervised by
Mary Ellen Cohn and Daniel Connors.
The book was designed by Noah's Art.
Typesetting was by Lincoln Graphics.

PHOTO CREDITS

Beverly Hall: pages 22, 25, 28, 44, 49, 52,
58, 62, 66, 68, 98, 105, 107, 108, 112,
114, 174.

Robert S. Halvey: page 26

Mel Wright: pages 130, 168

J.A. Loftus, SJ: pages 121, 124, 127, 134,
137, 139, 141, 154

Lee Pellegrini: Front Cover and pages 148, 153,
162, 164, 165, 166

Bob Desabaye: page 92

Christians have not hesitated to use every human art in their celebration of the saving work of God in Jesus Christ, although in every historical period they have been influenced, at times inhibited, by cultural circumstances. In the resurrection of the Lord, all things are made new. Wholeness and healthiness are restored, because the reign of sin and death is conquered. Human limits are still real and we must be conscious of them. But we must also praise God and give God thanks with the human means we have available. God does not need liturgy; people do, and people have only their own arts and styles of expression with which to celebrate.

FROM ENVIRONMENT AND ART IN CATHOLIC WORSHIP

Contents

PART 2 SHAPING LITURGICAL DANCE

PART 3 A VISION OF A DANCING CHURCH

Annotated Bibliography
Compiled by Gloria Weyman

Introduction

by Carla DeSola

Thio book fills a long felt gap in development of understanding between church people, liturgists and artists regarding the place of dance in worship. The authors delineate dance as a feature of religious life from the earliest origins in Judaism through subsequent centuries to the present. From deep personal experience, they discuss what dance has meant to their unique ministries, opening new dimensions of dialogue between liturgical dancers and those concerned with maintaining traditions of the church and its rich liturgical ritual. I was therefore deeply moved while reading Robert F. Ver Eecke's vision of a dancing church, Ronald G. Gagne's history of dance in the church, and Thomas Kane's careful development of categories of dance within the liturgy. Their contributions should serve well to clarify the role of liturgical dance in the Church and translate its possibilities for those who may never have considered dance as a way to God, facilitating human connectedness, love, and understanding.

A religious dancer is urged from within to respond to the richness of the feasts and seasons in the Church year. A dancer also has unique abilities to express experiences rooted in personal and intuitive levels into visible movement, transforming them publicly as part of the body of Christ in the liturgical worship of the Church.

All arts bring into focus what we directly experience in life but do not articulate. Art enables us to contemplate freshly a portion of the world in which we live. Dance connects us kinesthetically to more than our usual perceptions, thereby adding new dimensions to our lives. When the body is treated as sacrament, dance focuses peoples' attention on the now, and on the presence of God in space and time. The fleetingness of dance helps us to contemplate an instant in time — not just to look outward or to the future with longing, hope, or despair. Dance helps us experience the sacred in a moment — not "out there" but here, now, in present time and space. The simplicity underlying this is that dance, as a response to life, is a channel for the spirit to enter, stir the blood, and create anew hearts of flesh, not stone.

Movement is all around us, everyday, everywhere, and the sacred and profane are held together in the dimensions of space, time, rhythm, dynamic energy and beauty. From their spiritual depths, dancers can perceive such movement as expressions or manifestations of God's activity. It stimulates their sense of wonder and ignites their imagination, enabling them to transform images into kinesthetic responses of contraction and release, falling and rising, exalting in the mysterious peristalsis of the universe. Such perceptions enable dancers to hold together the silent beauty of a frozen landscape and a

future spring; perhaps as birds of the Spirit providing a vision to others of human potentialities for wholeness in body, mind and spirit.

Some examples may serve to illustrate the creative process: I recall a recent experience in which I was enriched while looking through frosted windows of a cabin in the forest on a snowy day. I suddenly recalled the old title, Our Lady of the Snows, and a vision of a dance formed in my mind of the "mother of mercy" reaching out for those lost in life's storms, leading them to the stillness of the forest in its winter form, correlating this with the need for stillness in the human soul. On another occasion, with the sun reflecting in a lake, a shaft of light reached me from the cold water. It reminded me that in the midst of coldness, I am God's child, beloved, and blessed with light, and that in the future I too can dance warmth into a psalm of thanksgiving for God's beloved earth. While viewing some paintings on the Stations of the Cross it occurred to me to incorporate in dance the concept of light diminishing and movement narrowing to an agonizing stop—the dance of the priest lying prostrate on Good Friday

I have been blessed in liturgical dance to have had many opportunities to creatively share in services in monasteries, retreat centers, schools, conventions and parishes as well as for ordinations, jubilees, first masses, installations, baptisms, and confirmations. My calling has also been highly ecumenical, sharing in services and events in numerous other church settings, including Episcopal, Methodist, Presbyterian, United Church of Christ, Unitarian, Quaker, Mennonite, Congregational, Lutheran, Interdenominational and Jewish Reformed services. These opportunities were concurrent with the renaissance of liturgical dance that followed Vatican II. It was fed by yearning shared by artists to contribute their talents to the living Church. During its recent evolution it has been nurtured by countless nuns, monks, liturgically minded pastors and lay persons within the Church. Concurrently, within Protestant churches, groups have formed to share their interest in movement, seeking to express their religious life more completely. The Sacred Dance Guild has been a center for much of this process and now has a considerable national membership.

Liturgical dance, within the Church, seeks to enrich worshipfulness and community participation in the mysteries as part of accepted rites. At times, dance so enhances liturgy that one cannot imagine a celebration without it. On other occasions it can be an intrusion. In its current stage of development, the state of the art is very fluid.

Presently, I perceive two main threads in liturgical dance: One relates to what can be called "folk" expression and the other is derived from disciplined and trained "classical" and modern dance sources. "Folk" expression attracts people who seek to share their religious feelings through communal movement, as in circle dances, uniform congregational movement, processions, simple prayer interpretation of psalms and dances derived from folk dance forms. In this folk art, people seek to free channels for fuller expression of the Spirit. On the other hand, "Fine Art" dance attracts serious and often highly trained dancers who seek to give well-rehearsed and choreographed expression to their visions both artistically and spiritually. In the fine arts, the standards of the art world are applied to the liturgical form, with the artist seeking to communicate spiritual values using the tools of the craft. I perceive a growing relationship between these two approaches, each being strengthened by contact with the other. One may state that devotional movement without training runs the risk of being uninspiring, poorly executed and distracting, but it can also be surprisingly pure and communally satisfying. Training without devotion, on the other hand, can prove unfruitful for the soul, but with increased spiritual depth can lead to experiences we truly hunger for. It is here that a third component is required, namely dancers having increasingly enriching opportunities to relate with liturgists. I believe it is in the exchange between artist and liturgist that the new art of liturgical dance is to be formed, as an inclusive art, greater than the sum of its parts.

Increasingly, in both Catholic and Protestant circles, dances performed by solo individuals, small dance ensembles or companies have been well done, and well received. There is a growing interest in having leaders of congregational movement who are able to collaborate fully with liturgists, ministers and other artists, particularly musicians. My experience is that inviting congregational movement is often perceived as more of a risk than having a solo dancer or trained dance company perform. However, when properly done, congregational movement becomes one of the most welcome and valued parts of liturgical worship, comparable with and as an aid to congregational singing.

Perhaps it is natural for a dancer to be able to adapt easily to many different settings and requirements. A dancer learns to work with diverse people. One learns to respond to other dancers, improvising jointly and sharing space and dancing in concert together. Dancers dance together whether they are Catholic, Protestant, Jewish or indeterminate. In this sense, dance goes beyond the rational and offers new experience and perhaps real hope as that which previously divided seems to diminish in a shared experience of power and healing. There is much to be explored on the ecumenical role of dance.

Each section of this book points to the future of liturgical dance, and each complements the others. Fr. Gagne writes vividly of the widespread Dance of Death in the Middle Ages, of the ring-dance of the angels, the dances at Easter, and dances held in the church yard to celebrate the victory of martyrs. They appear to constitute a tradition,

albeit intermittent, which we can draw upon. Fr. Kane gives tools to include modern liturgical dance today in our services. He categorizes dance according to its function in the liturgy. Fr. VerEecke points to the richness of the seasons as occasions for creation of liturgical danced prayers. Together they provide a framework and background for the continuing development of liturgical dance.

I would like to see liturgical dance develop on two levels:

(1) Individual parishes, or communities, enlisting to a much greater degree the talent of dancers from local communities.

(2) Development of dances to serve as *models* for church use throughout the country.

On the local level, parish liturgy committees would include dancers, and together they would develop local traditions of liturgical dance, as well as eliciting special dances for different occasions from the individual artist. An example of local tradition already in existence is the celebration of the Sundays of Advent—dancing with the Advent wreath, or with candles, usually to *O Come, O Come Emmanuel*. Perhaps we will eventually have a liturgical dance coordinator in a parish, filling a role similar to that of the music coordinator.

On the broader scene, we have a new tradition to forge by the development of dances that act as models for church use throughout the country. Eventually this could establish a tradition of religious dance, such as there was in the Middle Ages. I feel the next step will be for the Church to commission dance-rituals which speak of the problems of people today as did the great historical examples, cited previously, that grew out of the needs and spirituality of those times. To repeat, during the Middle-Ages the Dance of Death was performed all over Europe, taking different forms. Today we have an urgent need for a *Dance of Peace*. Perhaps Christmas would be the reason to develop and promulgate such a dance, using themes of light, Emmanuel, and the *Gloria* with its proclamation of peace on Earth (A modern-day ring-dance of the angels). The dance would be adapted according to the particulars of each Cathedral or church's resources, but eventually this would contribute to a tradition of religious dance that will really give vitality and an enfleshed expression to the prayers of our time.

Perhaps connected to this vision is the need for the formation of liturgical art centers or programs which draw dancers, musicians and liturgists together in dialogue, leading to collaboration, new works, and the setting of standards of competence and beauty that would benefit all.

At the present time, liturgical dance workshops are the common means of instruction and development in the field. Workshops have

been largely responsible for developing the art of liturgical dance. They have also been responsive to the need in many people for personal development both physically and spiritually. Workshops are often geared to encouraging dance for personal prayer, which leads naturally to a more articulate and knowing core of people who can stimulate and take responsibility to some extent in the local church. A sister who has attended my workshops recently wrote to me: "I'm looking to these hills, rocks, and mud, forest animals, stars and crisp chilly days to teach me about that kind of power and force working in me. I also look to dance to root that power in my body, express that power moving through my body, and let that power ease the tight hold my mind has on my body. It is a life-long agenda. . . ."

For a recent conference, I created a dance based on *The Diary of Anne Frank.* The conference was designed to further Christian and Jewish understanding. Anne Frank is a person who speaks to the hearts of so many people, Christians and Jews alike. In her diary she writes: ". . . I thank you, God, for all that is good and clear and beautiful, . . . I think about 'the good' going into hiding, of that which will come sometime; love, the future, happiness and of 'the beauty' which exists in the world; the world, nature, beauty and all, all that is exquisite and fine." St. Paul writes that "faith is the substance of things to be hoped for." Anne Frank is a bridge, a rainbow connecting the best in us. The Church is a bridge of love, of fullness, seeing, as Anne did, the evil in the world, but believing that evil is not the final word. Liturgical dance is a bridge, an ecumenical bridge that undercuts the differences words may give rise to, and speaks directly to the heart. Liturgical dance has the power to bring to light the shadows, fears, and undercurrents of emotion and despair that lie below the surface. It is an art form that witnesses to the human condition, living on a planet of unspeakable beauty, and faced today with the great task of understanding one another in a common love of life.

Carla De Sola
Director, Omega Liturgical Dance Company in residence at
Cathedral Church of St. John the Divine,
New York City

PART 1
Movement in
Cultic Prayer
Within the
Judaeo-Christian
Tradition

by Ronald G. Gagne, M.S.

CHAPTER 1

Cultic Movement in the Canaanite and Jewish Traditions

From the very inception of culture, thoughtful people have pondered the particularly deep, human meaning they saw embodied in the dance.[1] In fact, every advanced religion has had, or still has, dance as an essential part of its divine service or of its drama of mysteries.[2] Hugo Rahner states with little exaggeration that any scholar is rightfully compelled to admit that "in almost every century and in countless churches, a sacral dance, carried out both by clergy and laity, has been woven around the austere core of the liturgy."[3] This cultic dance always seems to have been joined very closely with song and music.[4] As Psalm 150 proclaims, "Praise him with lyre and harp, praise him with drums and dancing" (v. 3b, 4a).[5]

Just as dance has a depth for all to see, Mircea Eliade goes so far as to state that "All dances were originally sacred; in other words, they had an extrahuman model."[6] Lucian of Samosata wrote:

> . . . those who sketch the truest history of dancing would tell you that in the first generation of all things the dance grew up, appearing together with ancient Love. In fact, the circling motion of the stars and their intertwining with the fixed planets . . . are signs of the primaeval dance.[7]

Hugo Rahner suggests this somewhat by saying that ". . . in the dance there is cosmic mystery. It is an attempt to move in time with that creative love that 'made the sun and the other stars.' "[8] There is, in short, a depth and a mystery that the dance, and more specifically the cultic dance, emanates and proclaims. This depth is evidenced by all cultures, including the Jewish culture.

CANAANITE AND JEWISH PEOPLES

Before considering Jewish and Canaanite use of dance, some historical groundwork must be laid in order to place these peoples in proper perspective. This is necessary because, when the Jews invaded Canaan during the thirteenth century B.C., they were far removed from what we would term "conquerors" today.

Three points should be kept in mind about the Jewish people. They were, first of all, not a culturally creative people. Concerning such things as houses and household vessels, arts and crafts, the Jews were content to use the skill of others.[9] The Canaanites had already developed an advanced rural and urban life. Agriculture, commerce, and architecture had reached a high level.[10] Second, the Jews were nomadic whereas the Canaanites were of a higher, primarily agrarian culture. Therefore, agrarian feasts meant little to the Jews at the outset. And, third, the religion of Judaism at the time of the early settlement of Canaan was not unified but was comprised of three strands: one, the religion that the original settlers brought with them; another, the religious strain developed by the settled tribes that did not go down into Egypt; still another, the "Mosaic" religion given by special relevation to Moses and in turn imparted to the tribes whom he led out of Egypt.[11]

This "conquering" people both influenced and was influenced by the Canaanites whom it initially overpowered by force. The extent of the Canaanite influence shall be treated later in this section. The three points above will suffice for the present.

DANCE IN THE OLD TESTAMENT

In the Jewish traditions recorded in the Old Testament, it is safe to say that *"Almost all the references to dancing in the Old Testament concern occasions of worship."*[12] It is natural that the Jews ". . . should share in this common phenomenological feature of religion."[13] In Judaism, dancing was a common element in cultic worship. Evidences show that dancing was so common in worship that it can further be stated that ". . . *in many Old Testament passages alluding to cultic rejoicing but without explicit mention of dancing we can safely assume that dancing is implied.*"[14]

Although the sacred dance was used often to express the emotions and aspirations of the Jewish people, it does seem odd that there are so few passages in which dance is specifically mentioned in the Old Testament. If provision for ritual dancing was not included in all

the minutiae of the Mosaic legislation, then it might be correct to state
that dancing was not allowed. However, Dr. Oesterley in his old, but
revered study, *The Sacred Dance*,[15] points out that although Jewish
priestly historians and legislators did try to avoid major inferences to
heathen deities, it is doubtful that dance would have been summarily
excluded and forbidden. Dancing, for the Jewish people, was "a practice too deeply ingrained in human nature as a means of expressing
religious emotion to suggest that it implied assimilation to heathen
worship."[16] Dance was accepted and used in many worship situations
but was frequently not mentioned.

Some of the passages in which dance *was* mentioned give examples of the infectious excitement engendered and the exceedingly
proper joy expressed in dance to Yahweh. One of the most ancient
describes the jubilation following the safe passage of Israel through the
Red Sea: "Miriam, the prophetess, Aaron's sister, took up a timbrel,
and all the women followed her with timbrels, dancing. And Miriam
led them in the refrain: 'Sing of Yahweh: he has covered himself in
glory, horse and rider he has thrown into the sea' " (Ex.15:20-21).

King David danced in exultation before the Ark of God, "whirling
round before Yahweh with all his might" (2 Sam. 6:14). He was summarily judged to be foolish by Michal, the daughter of Saul, who was

watching from the window, as he whirled in his rotation dance.[17] When the Ark had finally reached its destination, David offered sacrifices, blessed the people, gave them gifts and allowed them to return home. Michal then approached David and chided him concerning his " 'displaying himself under the eyes of his servant-maids as any buffoon might display himself' " (v. 20). He answered her by saying " 'I was dancing for Yahwah, not for them . . . I shall dance before Yahweh and demean myself even more. In your eyes I may be base, but by the maids you speak of I shall be held in honor' " (v. 21-22). The author of the Book of Samuel both censured the hardness of Michal's heart and lauded the simplicity, earnestness, and blessed, foolish abandon with which David praises Yahweh.

In the Song of Songs (7: 1ff.), another type of dance, the wedding dance of a maiden, is described as graceful and beautiful. However, not all dancing was holy and acceptable in Yahweh's sight. In Exodus 32: 1-19, the passage describes the dance round the golden calf, which Moses condemned because of the people's idolatrous attitudes. (This seems to have been a giant ring-dance,[18] extremely common and referred to elsewhere in the Old Testament.)

The Book of Psalms also gives many examples of dances—cultic dances—because the psalms "are primarily cultic expressions of doctrine, . . . describing Yahweh as he was worshiped and experienced in

the liturgy. . . ."[19] The psalmist invites the assembly of Israel to: "Sing Yahweh a new song, let the congregation of the faithful sing his praise . . . let them dance in praise of his name, playing to him on strings and drums!" (Ps. 149: 1, 3.) One cannot help but catch the jubilant, festive excitement of the worshiping community. Some princes of other nations danced in joy before the Lord because they were recently declared freemen of the city: "And there will be princes dancing there. All find their home in you" (Ps. 87:7). So, again and again the psalms show their cultic nature.

PSALMS AND THE FEAST OF TABERNACLES

Some psalms cite more specific points of interest, which help this study. Psalm 118, for instance, describes a festival:

> Shouts of joy and safety
> in the tents of the virtuous.
> . . . .
> Open the gates of virtue to me,
> I will come in and give thanks to Yahweh.
> . . . .
> This is the day made memorable by Yahweh,
> what immense joy for us!
> . . . .
> We bless you from the house of Yahweh.
> . . . .
> With branches in your hands draw up in procession
> as far as the horns of the altar (v. 15, 19, 24, 26b, 27b).

This psalm around the altar speaks of a specific "day," the festival of Yahweh, thus indicating the Feast of Tabernacles.[20] On this day a person is heard joyfully pleading that the gates of the Temple be opened so all may process inside to dance around the altar, an accustomed feature of this feast.

The absorption of alien elements stands forth in Psalm 68. It commemorates Yahweh's saving deeds of the past, describing a mammoth procession with the Ark and finally Yahweh's enthronement in the Temple of Jerusalem. Important indications are noted by several commentators that this psalm indicates ". . . the taking over and adoption of an originally alien cultic tradition by the Yahweh cult, thus making evident the superiority and the power of absorption of Old Testament religion."[21]

Both Israel's adoption of alien cultic tradition, and the superior and transforming qualities of Israel's religion need further explanation to understand Israel's *special* use of dance in the cultic celebrations.

Therefore, the dancing during the Feast of Tabernacles and its similarities to the Canaanite New Year festival will be examined.

One important quality that seems to be an aspect of all Israelite festivals was rejoicing, an outlet for emotional expression and a time for relaxation.[22] The intensity with which the Israelites expressed and celebrated with their *whole being* is described by Helene de Lenval in this way:

> Highly conscious of its election, Israel maintained a personal relationship with God, and even as one human being communicates with another through the whole of himself, by thoughts, emotions, words, movements, tones of voice, so the people of the Bible employ their whole selves in their communication with their God. Easily moved and passionate, exuberant and impulsive, they express their feelings in a way which modern 'civilized' man may well find flamboyant. Struck down by misfortune, they weep, bewail themselves, tear out the hair of their beards, rend their garments and roll on the ground; in times of joy, they leap in the air, clap their hands, cry out, laugh and sing like children: and both their lamentations and their shouts of happiness are addressed to God.[23]

The Feast of Tabernacles, or Sukkoth, was the autumn feast, the "feast of ingathering," the most important and well-attended of the three annual pilgrimage feasts in Israel. It was referred to as *"the* feast" (1 Kgs. 8: 2, 65 and Ezech. 45: 25) and mentioned in the two most ancient calendars (Ex. 23:16 and 34: 22). The *Mishnah* refers to it by saying that ". . . whoever has not witnessed it has never seen a truly festive celebration."[24] Josephus referred to it as "a most holy and most eminent feast."[25]

In early Israel, this feast began as the ingathering of the harvest of the fields, (Ex. 23: 16), threshing-floor, and winepress (Deut. 16: 13). Somewhat later, it was associated with the passage through the desert during the Exodus (Neh. 8: 14 and referring to Lev. 23: 42-43) and became known as the feast of Huts ("tents" more properly).[26] The feast was originally not an Israelite institution but came from the Canaanite custom of celebrating an agricultural thanksgiving festival at the conclusion of harvest time. This the Israelites "adopted" or better yet "transformed"[27] without ever losing the agricultural character of the feast.[28]

Understanding the joy of this feast and the intensity with which the Israelites expressed their emotions, it should be no surprise that the word "feast" (hagg) originally denoted[29] that which was the essence of a festival: the sacred dance around the sanctuary. Any reference to dance, since it is presumed to be part of any festival, was considered to be superfluous and therefore mentioned infrequently.

Judges 21: 19-23 no doubt refers to this same feast when it describes the group-dancing done by maidens at "Yahweh's feast which is held every year at Shiloh" (v.19).

The evening torch dance at the water-pouring ceremony of the Feast of Tabernacles was also a custom and was recorded in Rabbinic tradition:

> It was said that the gladness there was above everything. Pious men danced with torches in their hands and sang songs of joy and praise, while the Levites played all sorts of instruments. The dance drew crowds of spectators for whom grandstands had been erected. It did not end until the morning at a given sign, when water from the spring of Shiloh was poured over the altar.[30]

This does not appear to be a custom of later Jewish times but rather an old revered tradition[31] of exuberant community celebration.

The Israelites were certainly affected by the religion (and customs) of the Canaanites whom they conquered. The similarities between the Canaanites' and the Israelites' celebration of the New Year festival (Tabernacles) are many, including their music, dances, and songs.[32] In the Jews' assimilation of elements of the Canaanite New Year feast, the primary meaning of the feast was not lost in the process. It was still an occasion for thanksgiving and rejoicing in the gifts (of Yahweh) seen in the yearly harvest. An important innovation began when, as stated in Lev. 23: 42-43, the feast ". . . took on significance as a commemoration of Yahweh's leading the Israelites through the desert to the Promised Land."[33] This shows a process of "assimilation" to be present, thus positing a connection between a primitive ritual (i.e., the feast of Tabernacles) and an historical event from Israel's past (i.e., the Exodus event).[34] This supported a teleological outlook (namely that everything has an historical purpose), as opposed to a cyclic view of life and of God's actions in history. The Israelite tribes thus acquired the sense of common ancestry and a divinely guided past.[35] They now saw new meaning in celebrating the Feast of Tabernacles.

Through the conflict between the old views of Israel and the religion of the "conquered" Canaanites, this historical Yahwism helped Israel to become conscious of the inherent peculiarities and potentialities of their religion and to expand them.[36] Thus the feast came to mean: sacred fertility rites (Canaan) vs. purity of life and renewal of Yahweh's promise of power (Israel); gross mythology and idols as gods (Canaan) vs. the God of history, nature, and humankind (Israel); the gods of the peoples (Canaan) vs. the God of Israel; the gods who come to life again vs. the God who always lives, and creates life out of God's own life (Israel).[37]

DANCE AND YAHWEH

In short, while in the process of discovering more about the God of its ancestors, Israel found out more and more about itself, its possibilities, its limitations, and was open to new ways in which God could communicate with God's people. An early form of prophetism with which they dealt well was a phenomenon common among their neighbors. An example of this is found in 1 Sam. 10: 5b-7:

> . . . and as you come to the town you will meet a group of prophets coming down from the high place, headed by harp, tambourine, flute and lyre; they will be in an ecstasy. Then the spirit of Yahweh will seize on you, and you will go into an ecstasy with them, and be changed into another man. When these signs are fulfilled for you, act as occasion serves, for God is with you.

In this passage, the prophets performed this dance, allowing God's power to overwhelm them and take them prisoner. They could see how dancing could be a way of readying themselves to receive the spirit of Yahweh.[38] This type of sacred dance, although mentioned only a few times in the Old Testament, seems to be nothing out of the ordinary in the years that followed.[39]

Dance, as Israel discovered, can express yearning and openness to Yahweh. It can actually be a vehicle, as in the case of Saul, through which the spirit of Yahweh can truly seize and change people with Yahweh's power and love. Yet, there were (and are) those who would tend to "spiritualize" dance perhaps because they feel that ". . . the Power of the Dance is a dangerous power. Like other forms of self-surrender, it is easier to begin than to stop."[40]

CHAPTER 2

Cultic Movement in the First Two Centuries of the Christian Church

The early Christian Church is most important in the understanding of the Christian tradition. As might be suspected from the treatment of the Canaanite influence on the Jews of old, similarly ". . . the figures of Christ and the Church assume their proper significance only in the light of the divine realities already present in Palestinian Judaism."[41]

SITUATION OF THE EARLY CHURCH

Cultic movement in the first two centuries of the Christian Church is difficult to trace due to the lack of source material specifically treating the crucial first century. The few references to cultic movement necessitate that the approach be one of inferences drawn from parallels of other appropriations of Jewish elements by the Christian Church, specifically in the case the Feast of Tabernacles in the early Church. What follows is a picture of the situation in which the early Church found itself.

The disciples of Jesus lived in a culture which abounded in cultic traditions formed in ages past. Two important cultic traditions at this time were the Temple at Jerusalem and the synagogues of the diaspora. How they affected the cultic life of the early Church and how they too eventually evolved is the first consideration.

Briefly stated, the splendid Temple at Jerusalem was for the Jews both a symbol of Yahweh's gratuitous choice of Israel as his own people and (at least from 538 B.C. to 70 A.D.) the unique place of worship for all of Judah. Joseph Bonsirven recounts some of the affectionately exaggerated legends which indicate the pride and admiration with which the people viewed their Temple and the grand scale of their worship of Yahweh.

> The odor of its spices caused goats to sneeze for many miles around; on the feast of Sukkoth it challenged the illumination of the sun, and all of Jerusalem was as bright as daylight; the noise caused by the opening of the Temple gates awakened the whole city. These stories are simply the popular and naive expression of the love people had for their unique Temple.[42]

The joyous tenor of their celebrations with much dancing and music especially during the Feast of Tabernacles (Sukkoth) has already been shown.

TEMPLE AND SYNAGOGUE

The greatest and certainly the unique creation of Judaism was the Synagogue.[43] Its creation meant a religious revolution but not in the sense that Jews became dissaffected with their Jerusalem Temple.[44] "In principle, there was certainly nothing in this innovation hostile to the Temple; the synagogue was rather its complement . . ."[45] The special function of the Synagogue was the dissemination among the Jews (especially of the diaspora) of the particular kind of religious instruction that was necessary for their understanding and proper observance of the many requirements of the Law.[46]

The great tendency in speaking of the Temple-Synagogue relationship is to place them in opposition.

> But modern scholarship, especially the researches of the Scandinavian scholars, has demonstrated the fallacy of opposing the religion of the synagogue as a religion of the word to the religion of the Temple as a ritual religion. It has shown that the origin of the religion of the word was in the ritual religion of Israel, the religion of the Temple itself, and, before the Temple existed, the religion of the other sanctuaries, to which the guilds of prophets were attached from the beginning. Reciprocally whatever may have been the importance of reading God's word in the synagogal worship, the synagogue has never become just a kind of religious school-room.[47]

Jesus himself was a part of this tradition of attachment to the Word and God's presence in the Temple.[48] Yet, as Professor Bartlet observes,

Jesus' own example and teaching are associated with the synagogal type of worship rather than with the Temple, the seat of the sacrificial and priestly system of worship. For to Him the Temple was primarily "a house of prayer," and that private (Lk. xviii. 10) rather than public prayer. Indeed the latter hardly seems to be alluded to by Jesus at all (not even in Matt. xviii. 19). His teaching on worship is mainly on genuine prayer, as opposed to formal prayers, "vain repetitions" (Matt. vi. 5ff., cp. Lk. xviii. 10-14); and even "the Lord's Prayer" is given as an example of prayer of the right sort rather than as a form for regular repetition.[49]

Singing with its usual accompanying dances was not a part of the synagogal worship. This does not bode well for dance in the New Testament Church celebrations.

DANCE IN THE NEW TESTAMENT

Dance is referred to very few times in the New Testament. But even this points to the possible parallel of the Jewish tradition of presuming the presence of dance without the need to mention it explicitly. Certainly the spontaneity and enthusiasm engendered by the influence of the Holy Spirit could possibly urge this presumption. Always keeping in mind David's dance before the Ark and Miriam's dance after crossing the Red Sea, the New Testament underlines the importance of dance in the adoration and worship of God. Matthew refers rather obliquely to dancing through Jesus' remark: " 'What description can I find for this generation? It is like children shouting to each other as they sit in the market place: 'We played the pipes for you, and you wouldn't dance; we sang dirges,' and you wouldn't be mourners' " (Mt. 11: 16-17). Both Matthew and Luke (7: 32) place this in the context of the Jews' rejection of both Jesus' message and that of John the Baptist, his precursor. The idea put forth by both evangelists could be either: first, that the children could get no response whatever from their playmates (paralleling Jesus and the Baptist vs. the uninterested Jews) or second, that the Jews wanted to play games, to dance and to wail, yet Jesus and John the Baptist would not do this at the whim and fancy of the Jews. Following either interpretation however, dancing was not the reason for rejection. It was rather the aimlessness or foolishness exhibited by some of the Jewish nations. Dance in praise of Yahweh was certainly not discouraged.

An echo of the condemnation of the pagan cultic amusement and dancing before the golden calf (Ex. 32: 6, 19) can be paralleled in 1 Cor. 10:7 as Paul cautions his hearers concerning the actions of the Jews of old: "Do not become idolaters as some of them did, for the scripture says: 'After sitting down to eat and drink, the people got up to amuse themselves . . .' " (i.e., shameless dancing and possibly cultic licentiousness[50]). Another rather oblique but favorable reference to dancing, referring to dancing in the Spirit, is found in 2 Cor. 12: 2 in which Paul tries to describe how he was elevated in ecstasy. Backman proposes: "Perhaps it implies that when St. Paul found himself in the Heavenly Paradise he must have also participated in the celestial mysteries, to which especially belonged the round-dances of the saints and angels."[51] In connection with this, Backman further states that: "At an unusually early stage, possibly even as early as the establishment of the Christian community, the dance was described as one of the heavenly joys and as a part of the adoration of the divinity by the angels and by the saved."[52] It has also been attested to that "Dancing still took place in the temple courtyard in New Testament times, on the Feast of Tabernacles."[53]

FEAST OF TABERNACLES: NEW TESTAMENT ERA

Before treating what the Fathers of the Church and other Christian writers said about dancing in New Testament times, an examination of the Feast of Tabernacles as found in the New Testament will help show how this feast was transformed and carried into the early Church from Judaism. This tendency is found again in the Church Fathers' writings on cultic dance.

The Feast of Tabernacles has no strict equal in the liturgical life of the early or present-day Christian Church. The reason for this is that Christ "reread" and "relived" this Feast. The result of this "reliving" is the spiritualization of the Feast by the New Testament writer, translating the Feast into New Testament typology. A more heightened eschatological framework was built around the Feast. An example of this is explained by David M. Stanley, when he states that ". . . the evangelists' accounts of the Transfiguration seem to indicate that, in their eyes and that of the apostolic Church, this mystery [of Transfiguration] was the fulfillment of the liturgical symbolism of the greatest of all Israelite feasts, that of Tabernacles."[54] In the Transfiguration event (Mk. 9: 2-8; Mt. 17: 1-8; Lk. 9: 28-36) the offer to "make three tents" (Mk. 9: 5) certainly parallels the huts of the Feast. In the Gospel of John, there are additional parallels to the Feast that bring out Christ as the fulfillment of the Feast. Jean Danielou says that John 12: 12-19 (the procession of palms and the singing of two verses of Psalm 118,[55] greeting Jesus' triumphal entry into Jerusalem) ". . . signifies that the coming of the Messiah, prefigured by the solemn procession of the seventh day of the Feast of Tabernacles, is fulfilled in the person of Jesus."[56] In the Book of Revelation, John also uses the liturgy of the Feast of Tabernacles to describe the procession of the elect around the heavenly altar (Rev. 7: 9-17). Fr. Danielou points out the details connected with the Feast: palm-branches held in

their hands, the white robes (as in Transfiguration), the tent God
spreads over the elect, the springs of living water where they quench
their thirst (as in ablutions on the last day of the Feast). Other scholars
see still more parallels.[57]

The spiritualizing of the Feast of Tabernacles by Christ according
to New Testament writers and the resultant absence of the Feast *per se*
in the Christian liturgical calendar show that ". . . the life it celebrated
was not sufficiently a life born of death; the harvest it extolled was not
sufficiently the fruit of the seed dying in the earth."[58] Christ has made
a difference. No longer is the divine presence bound to the beautiful
Temple, but rather to the Person of Christ. Worship is no longer in a
place, but in the spirit.[59] While the Feast itself did not survive,
elements of the Feast certainly may have been also a part of the yearly
calendar of celebration for the emerging early Church.

The process of separation from—yet continuity with—Judaic
customs experienced by the first Jewish Christians is an interesting
one and important for the understanding of the place of dance in the
New Testament tradition and in the early Church. At the outset, Jewish
Christians expected nothing other than to worship in the Synagogues.
But when tension grew, they naturally formed their own
Synagogues.[60] Whatever happened on the sabbath morning, all the
Christians, Jew and Gentile alike, were expected to meet for a meal
and the breaking of the bread on Saturday (the Sabbath) evening as
Paul mentions in 1 Cor. 11: 17-34. Concerning the Matthaean church

community in particular, Michael Goulder states that:

> we may depend (on the fact) that the Matthaean church, struggling to maintain its orthodoxy, . . . followed the Jewish Calendar, with its feasts and fasts, and that the lections used (were) . . . the Jewish lections. . . . What we *should* expect by way of a change is a series of Christian readings which showed how the Law and the Prophets had been fulfilled.[61]

He finds these Christian readings for the eight-day-Feast of Tabernacles in Matthew 13:1-16:12.[62]

In this context of continuity with Judaic customs, dance would seem to have a natural place in Synagogue worship. And since the model of the *Synagogue* remained part of the worship of the early Church, the Synagogue paradoxically became an important vehicle in spreading the message of Christianity (and this new blend of customs) far and wide.[63] There were two significant limiting factors for the use of dance by the early Church. First, simple availability of space had to be reckoned with because they now used smaller Synagogues and broke bread together in private homes. Second, their tendency to spiritualize elements of Jewish tradition may have affected their use of dance.

FATHERS OF THE EARLY CHURCH AND DANCE

During this post-testamental period of the early Church, various changes are evident. The specific changes with regard to the form of the Mass are perceivable from the meager sources available. These changes are important in the appreciation of Christianity's adaptation within the New Dispensation. For example, Justin the Martyr, in his *First Apology*, written about the year 150 A.D., gave clear evidence that the Christian service of reading, sermon, and prayer (modeled on the Sabbath morning Service) was for the first time joined to the celebration of the Mass.[64] Also during this time, perhaps *the* greatest change in the whole course of the history of the Mass took place: namely, the abandonment of the meal as a setting for Mass. This change was urged and necessitated both by the impracticality of increasing numbers of Christians gathering (in a previously domestic situation) around a table and also by the gradual enrichment of the prayer of thanksgiving. By the end of the first century, what the Christians celebrated was referred to as "the Eucharist" rather than "the breaking of the bread,"[65] thus emphasizing a different aspect of the celebration.

By the end of the second century, Christian writers were stressing more and more the spiritual, "thanksgiving" character of Christian worship, putting themselves in opposition to the pagans' emphasis on sacrifice or even the Jews' emphasis on the physical action, the outward gift.[66] This same tendency (to oppose and spiritualize) became evident in the changing view of dance as cultic prayer. Yet in this second century, Lucian of Samosata, in true Platonic thought-patterns, stated that dance is the moment's attempt to express the harmony between the body and the soul. He further said "Dance is not merely a pleasure; it is an act good for the soul," the interpretation of what is hidden in the soul.[67]

The Christian writers of these first three centuries tried to deal with all the following: opposition to the pagans; separation from the Jews of old; formation of their lives within the New Dispensation, while always trying to remain true to their biblical roots (remembering the dances of Miriam and David). The resulting tensions will surface, and opinions will solidify.

Around the years 130-150 A.D., the famous *Shepherd of Hermas* appeared, containing a number of similes of a secret and symbolic nature. This document describes how Hermas visited God's holy mountain, his dwelling place. There Hermas met twelve white-robed virgins, holy and spotless. They received him warmly. And he says that they began to ". . . lead me round the tower, and to play with me. And I, too, became like a young man, and began to play with them: for some of them formed a chorus, and others danced, and others sang; and I, keeping silence, walked with them around the tower, and was merry with them."[68] From this selection, It is evident that as early as the first third of the second century, the dance was seen as a fitting part of celestial bliss.[69]

Clement of Alexandria, 150-216 A.D., in his *Address to the Heathens* states:

> I will show thee the Word, and the mysteries of the Word, expounding them after thine own fashion. This is the mountain beloved of God, . . . and there revel on it . . . daughters of God, the fair lambs, who celebrate the holy rites of the Word, raising a sober choral dance. The righteous are the chorus; the music is a hymn of the King of the Universe. . . . O truly sacred mysteries! O stainless light! My way is lighted with torches, and I survey the heavens and God; I become holy whilst I am initiated. . . . Such are the reveries of my mysteries. If it is thy wish, be thou also initiated; and thou shalt join the choir along with angels around the unbegotten and indestructible and the only true God, the Word of God, raising the hymn with us.[70]

Backman takes the last image (join in the choral dance around God) quite literally, suggesting that they be seen as having a double meaning. He suggests that physical dancing in the present time is more than a reference to future dance with the angels of heaven. When persons dance on earth they also dance with the angels. They can rightfully be all the more joyous, knowing that they are in the company of both the faithful saints on earth and the holy angels of heaven.

Clement speaks of the occasion of the "reveries of my mysteries," meaning the celebration of entrance or initiation into the Church through the sacraments. This joyful entrance was actually done in Clement's time to the accompaniment of torches, song, and the ring-dance,[71] possibly referring back to the torch-dance around the altar during the Feast of Tabernacles. (In later years, Ambrose requested that persons about to be baptized approach the font dancing.[72])

Again, Clement in his *Stromata* mentions the prevalent custom of bodily movement during prayer. "Therefore we raise our heads and our hands to heaven (during prayer) and move our feet just at the end of the prayer. . . . we seek by words of prayer to raise our body above the earth and uplift the winged soul by its desire for better things."[73] Dance was still a vibrant part of their prayer.

With *Apostolic Tradition* of Hippolitus of Rome, written about 215 A.D., for the first time there is evidence of an emergence of an order in prayer: an order of laws regulating clergy and the conduct of liturgical functions and evidence of an order of rites and ceremonies to be observed by clergy and laity.[74]

The description of the Bridegroom in the *Canticle of Canticles* speaks of his light airy movements: "I hear my Beloved, See how he comes leaping on the mountains, bounding over the hills. My Beloved is like a gazelle, like a young stag . . ." (2: 8-9a). Perhaps after reading this, Hippolytus was inspired to write his great Easter hymn of praise:

> O thou leader of the mystic round-dance! O divine Pasch and new feast of all things! O cosmic festal gathering! O joy of the universe, honour, ecstasy, exquisite delight by which dark death is destroyed . . . and the people that were in the depths arise from the dead and announce to all the hosts of heaven: "The thronging choir from earth is coming home."[75]

He speaks further of these Christian mysteries and connects them with dancing.

> O these great mysteries! What is meant by this 'leaping'? The Logos leapt from heaven into the womb of the Virgin, he leapt from the womb of his mother on to the cross, from the cross into Hades and from Hades once more back onto the earth — O the new resurrection! And he leapt from the earth into heaven where he sits on the right hand of the Father. And he will again leap on to the earth with glory to bring judgment.[76]

Hippolytus connected the dancing figures of the Old Testament with the allegorical dances of the Christ, which no doubt helped to break down the inhibitions of his contemporaries in continuing such customs as the dance to the baptismal font.

Another Church Father, Gregory the Wonder-Worker, 213-270 A.D., is said to have extended the use of the dance in connection with the memorial festivals for the martyrs. This supposition is strengthened by the following passage:

> He who has done everything preserved and proscribed by Providence in its secret mysteries, reposes in Heaven in the bosom of the Father and in the cave in the bosom of the Mother (Christ Jesus). The ring-dance of the angels encircles him, singing his glory in Heaven and proclaiming peace on earth.[77]

Gregory has suggested to the ages of Christians to come that faith sees in death merely a change, a passage to the joys of heaven. Why should believers not dance on earth while the angels do the ring-dance for the martyrs who have at last returned home, having completed their pilgrimage back to the Father? For Gregory the Wonder-Worker, dance can expand not only the bodies and minds but above all deepen the faith of those still on earth.

CONSTANTINE THE GREAT

During the fourth century, significant changes took place both within and outside of the Christian Church. One major cause of change was the presence of Constantine I, the Great, Roman Emperor. During his reign (306-337 A.D.) he was instrumental in accepting and firmly supporting the Christian Church in the Roman Empire. Constantine converted to Christianity in 312 A.D. and in October of that same year defeated Maxentius, his rival in Rome. Soon afterward, he had himself proclaimed senior Augustus by the Roman Senate. During the following year, he met with his co-emperor, Licinius, at Milan. They both agreed to grant equality of rights to all religions. However, they issued no formal edict, presumably to avoid premature interference with Maximin Daia, their counterpart in the East.

Constantine officially recognized the Christian bishops as counselors of the state, and gradually extended juridical rights to all of them. As attested to in the Theodosian Code (1.27.1), in 318 A.D. he gave legal force to the bishops' solution of civil suits and by 321 A.D. both permitted the emancipation of slaves in church and recognized bequests to the Church (16.2.4). Constantine made Sunday a civil holiday and (2.8.1) freed Christian soldiers for religious services. He also opened the Council of Nicea (June of 325 A.D.) to foster peace and unity in both Church and Empire. Although he did continue his toleration of paganism, his laws were gradually influenced by the Christian ethic, thus affecting the whole of the Empire.[78]

CHRISTIANITY AND CHANGE

This period was a time of great change for the early Church. Legally, the Church, once an enemy of the state, was now formally accepted. Where it had been perilous to be known as a Christian, membership in the Church now became fashionable and advantageous. Concerning worship, coming from small private domestic gatherings, the Church was now given Sunday as its day to worship. And for their worship, due to the vast numbers of conversions, they sought the use of giant basilicas to house their congregations. However, these changes evidenced a change in their views.

Through the clergy's close identity with the state at this time, the fourth century brought a rise in triumphalism. This can be seen in the buildings either constructed or merely used as churches. Louis Bouyer points out that when the Christians of the second century (and earlier) desired to worship, they gathered in the homes of friendly patricians. The priest sat among the people.[79] Due to Constantine's open support of Christianity, the growing groups of Christians burst the confines of the home and began to use the old dignified, spacious basilicas—Roman business halls. As grandiosity was introduced (at least architecturally) into Christian worship, it fostered a change in attitudes that brought about a gradual and partial erosion of the spirit of Christian worship. For example, the seat of the bishop was moved from the center of the room (in the patrician home-worship situations) to the apse of the basilica, near the far wall. The altar was brought to the center, the nave, where all the worshiping community gathered, at least for the second part of the liturgy. The seat of the bishop became the throne, using the same placement as the emperor's chair in the Roman Senate. It is true that bishops had become authorities of the state, but this new liturgical placement supported the view that the bishops were

> . . . to be regarded as authorities above and outside the Church, rather than an authority in the Church linked with her collective life. Hence the new separation, instead of a mere distinction, between clergy and faithful, was completely unknown in the primitive Christian worship, as well as previously in the synagogue.[80]

Later, another modification was to alter much more deeply the character of the primitive celebration of the early Church.

> Then not only would the bishop and the clergy be removed from the congregation for the first part of the service, but they would remain in their lofty isolation even for the eucharist. For the altar itself would come to be moved to their own exclusive precinct.[81]

This change was even more radical, allowing that the new and special quality of Christian worship was open to compromise. The specific ". . . uniqueness of Christian worship was not just the type of relationship it established with the divinity but the new relationship it created among people—a relationship that was one of mutual love and service."[82]

With all these changes in the first two centuries of Christianity (especially the evolution of worship from Temple and Synagogue to home and finally to basilica, with dance being more readily associated with celestial bliss), cultic dance was still acceptable because it was planted deep in the soil of the Judaeo-Christian tradition. But circumstances in the fourth and subsequent centuries brought more changes regarding the importance and meaning of dance.

CHAPTER 3

Cultic Movement in Liturgical Prayer From the Fourth Century to the Present

During the crucial fourth century, the situation of the Christian Church changed immensely. This chapter indicates how the Church's view toward dance changed from the fourth century to the present. This is indeed a massive task. This analysis will concentrate especially on the Fathers of the Church in the fourth to the sixth centuries, summarizing the remaining centuries through a brief overview of the decisions of the Councils and Synods of the Church concerning liturgical dance. The Chronology at the end of this section lists the major events and statements which shaped the use of dance, and graphically indicates the positive and negative influences.

FOURTH-CENTURY WRITERS

Chapter two concluded with Constantine I's changing the situation of Christianity in the Empire. Eusebius of Caesarea (264?-339 A.D.) tells of the way Christians danced to glorify God after the famous victory of Constantine:

> All fear therefore of those who had formerly afflicted them was taken away from men, and they celebrated splendid and festive days. Everything was filled with light, and those who before were downcast beheld each other with smiling faces and beaming eyes. With dances and

hymns, in city and country, they glorified first of all God the universal King, because they had been thus taught, and then the pious emperor with his God-beloved children.[83]

Eusebius' statement emphasizing that the Christian *first* gave glory to God by their dance was no doubt an effort to avoid any possible hint of pagan practices of dancing.

Backman cites a sermon written in the early years of the fourth century about the festival of Polyeuctes, a famous early Christian martyr. The author is unknown but the passage documents an interesting fact:

> Today we stand here in memory of his divine anniversary; it is granted to us to appreciate his noble deeds, and it is the duty of the faithful among Christians to proclaim them everywhere. But what can we offer to the martyr that is worthy of him. By what acts of grace can we return the love which he bore for God? If you so wish, then let us in his honor perform our customary dances.[84]

This is the first indication that religious dances were "customarily" performed at the burial place of the martyr or near the relics.

Also, it is not until the beginning of this century that there is unquestionable evidence that dancing was done in a Christian churchyard or sanctuary. However it is important to remember that before this period the Church did not use such expansive buildings — dancing in domestic homes or yards being a rather restricted possibility. The evidence of churchyard dancing comes in a decree from the Provincial Synod of Elvira (300-303 A.D.) in Spain. The Synod decision ordered ". . . that women should not be permitted to hold night watches in churchyards, at which, under the cloak of prayer, they [fall] into sin.[85]

SPIRITUALIZATION OF DANCE

Church dances began to show occasional signs of degeneration. Drinking and loose living crept into Church festivals. Women were taking a more active part and men and women were dancing together, a heretofore unseen happening at Church-related festivals.[86] The cautious and dubious struggle with the Church dance is evident in the writings of Epiphanius (315-403 A.D.), a bishop in Cyprus who sought to *spiritualize* the dance. His enthusiastic description of how the Palm Sunday festival should be conducted urged persons to "Rejoice, be glad and leap boisterously thou all-embracing Church! For behold, once again the King approaches . . . let us dance the choral dance before the pure Bridegroom as befits the divine bridegroom." But he concluded by saying, "Celebrate thy festival, thou Christian Church, not in the letter, not performing the ring dance in the physical sense, but in the spiritual, perceiving the destruction of the false gods and the setting up of the Church.[87] Most of the Fathers of the Church in this time showed this same tendency. In certain circumstances, they attempted to turn their eyes away from the actual, physical movement intrinsic to dance and regard dance from a singularly spiritualized perspective, as symbolic of spiritual motions of the soul.[88]

FATHERS OF THE CHURCH

The Fathers of the Church certainly struggled with the physical and spiritual aspects of the dance. They struggled, trying to reconcile the biblical evidence with their own lived experience. Even the rather sober Jerome (340-420 A.D.) could not help but recognize that prayerful dance was good and essentially joyful: "In the Church the joy of the spirit finds expression in bodily gesture and her children shall say with David as they dance the solemn step: 'I will dance and play before the face of the Lord.' "[89] They saw this joy as anticipation of celestial bliss.

Basil the Great (344-407 A.D.), Bishop of Caesarea, thoroughly approved of church dances. In letter 40, he spoke of one who had died in blessedness: "We remember those who now, together with the Angels, dance the dance of the Angels around God, just as in the flesh they performed a spiritual dance of life and, here on earth, a heavenly dance."[90] He even described life here on earth as a spiritual heavenly dance: "Could there be anything more blessed than to imitate on earth the ring-dance of the angels and at dawn to raise our voices in prayer and by hymns and songs glorify the rising Creator."[91] Yet with all his praise of dance, Basil was still shocked at the base sensuality, the frivolous and indecent movements, the lewd songs of the women who participated in the Easter dances. His position is clear:

> Casting aside the yoke of service under Christ . . . they . . . shamelessly attract the attention of every man. With unkempt hair, clothed in bodices and hopping about, they dance with lustful eyes and loud laughter; as if seized by a kind of frenzy they excite the lust of the youths. They execute ring-dances in the churches of the Martyrs and at their graves, instead of in the public buildings, transforming the Holy places into the scene of their lewdness. With harlots' songs they pollute the air and sully the degraded earth with their feet in shameful postures.[92]

In this passage, Basil clearly does not condemn dance in church but, rather, specific circumstances in which the explicitly sexual dimension is displayed with flagrant abandon.

Like Jerome and Basil, Ambrose (340-397 A.D.) took his cue for church dance from the Scriptures. Concerning the passage about David (2 Sam 6:14), he says that David

> . . . played before the Lord as his servant and . . . She who censured such dancing was condemned to barrenness and had no children by the king . . .

Further on he speaks of Matthew 11:17:

> The Jews who did not dance and knew not how to clap their hands were abandoned, but the Gentiles were called and applauded God in spirit . . . This is the wise man's honorable dance which David danced, mounting by the loftiness of his spiritual dance to the throne of Christ . . .[93]

Ambrose felt that those who view church dance must view the actions "under the aspect of holy religion." Then the dance will become truly reverential. Those people (like Michal) who censure these actions ". . . drag their own souls into the net of censure."[94] In other words, Ambrose preferred to define dance as "spiritual applause" but certainly did not rule out the physical church dance. After all, he was the one who suggested dancing before the font of one's baptism.[95] But dancing without doing this "under the aspect of holy religion" (that is, doing it to excess, carelessly or immorally) was as much to be condemned as the dance of Herodias' daughter, which secured the Baptist's death.[96] The process of attempting to spiritualize the church dance gained more momentum due to the abuses encountered by Ambrose and his contemporaries.

It is a great distance from the Milan of Ambrose to the Constantinople of Gregory, but attitudes with regard to dance were similar. Gregory also saw great value in dance, yet he tried to be prudent when he said: ". . . do not dance the dance of the shameless Herodias. . . . if you must dance, . . . dance the dance of David before the ark of God, for I believe that such a dance is the mystery of the sweet motion and nimble gesture of one who walks before God."[97] The churchyard festivals of song and dance for the martyrs were prevalent at this time in Constantinople. According to Gregory, these festivals involved a threefold benefit: "the suppression of the devils, avoidance of disease and knowledge of things to come."[98] The dances were seen as therapeutic: devils and vices were trampled underfoot, people were delivered from the powers of the underworld. All these are appropriate results of the Dance of the Angels.

Gregory of Nyssa (335-394 A.D.), was the last of the three great

Cappadocians, the others being Basil the Great and Gregory of Nazianzen (Gregory of Nyssa being the brother of Basil). In his *Homily on the Psalms*, Gregory of Nyssa saw Jesus as the One and Only Choreographer (somewhat akin to Hippolytus' Jesus who is "the One Who Leaps to save us").[99] The homily he wrote on Psalm 52 (Septuagint version) told of the blessed dance at the end of life, just as it was in the Paradise of Eden:

> Once there was a time when the whole of rational creation formed a single dancing chorus looking upwards to the one leader of this dance. And the harmony of that motion which was imparted to them by reason of his law found its way into their dancing.[100]

But original sin destroyed this dance-like harmony. At the end of time, all harmony will be restored and the believers will "dance in the ranks

of the angelic spirits" if they do not "succumb in the battle of temptation."[101] Here too the tendency toward spiritualization of dance is
seen.

Another Bishop of Constantinople, John Chrysostom (345-407
A.D.), did not mince words when he spoke of dancing. His *Homily on
Matthew* left absolutely no doubt as to his opinion. In speaking of
Herodias' daughter, he stated:

> For *where dancing is, there is the evil one*. For neither did God give us
> feet for this end, but that we may walk orderly: not that we may behave
> ourselves unseemly, not that we may jump like camels (for even they too
> are disagreeable when dancing, much more women), but that we may
> join the choirs of angels.[102]

With John Chrysostom, Augustine (354-430 A.D.), Bishop of Hippo,
was in full accord. He regarded dance as bringing one's bodily
members in accord with the love of God.[103] In his true pastoral concern, Augustine preached a sermon that attempted to help his people
appreciate dance on a spiritual plane. The background for this sermon
is that is was delivered in Carthage on St. Cyprian's day in the great
basilica. Each year festivities spilled over even into the basilica itself.
Loose songs and gay dancing were frequent. In this context Augustine
began with the quote "We have sung and you have not danced." He
asked what this meant. Then he continued: "He sings who commands.
He dances who obeys. What else is dancing but following sounds,
with the motions of the body? . . . In our case dancing means changing the manner of our life." Augustine stated that Cyprian was the
leader in this dance but

> . . . when God called the tune, he hearkened and began to dance—not
> with the motions of his body but with those of the soul. He adapted
> himself to this good music, this new music, he followed it: he loved and
> he endured, he fought and he conquered.[104]

Apparently this sermon did not have a lasting effect because, on a vigil
of another feast, just before Mass Augustine requested a bishop to
drive the singing and dancing mob out of the basilica. The worshipers
were in an uproar yet Augustine stood by his difficult decision. They
were to enter the church once again but in silence.[105] In another sermon, he quickly dismissed the subject by insisting that "the martyrs
did not go dancing to their death, but with prayers upon their
lips. . ."[106]

The problems the Fathers were having with dance were not sub-
siding. The constant rise in the number of converts made their efforts
seem all the more needed but fruitless because the newly converted

pagans were making great attempts to retain the dances of their own pagan cults.

Caesarius of Arles (470-542 A.D.) was most forthright in his condemnation of dancing at the vigils of martyrs' feasts. He stated that a person is not really a Christian if he executes ". . . dances and pantomimes before the very churches of the saints . . . because that kind of dancing has carried over from pagan practices." For Caesarius, cultic dancing was a ". . . most sordid and disgraceful act." [107]

CULTIC DANCE: EARLY MIDDLE AGES

Beginning well before Caesarius' time, the historical records concerning cultic dance consist mostly of ecclesiastical censures. The Church in the Early Middle Ages (300—1100 A.D.) was caught between her desire to evangelize and her need to deal with the cultures and practices of her converted brethren. By the time of Pope Gregory the Great (590-604, A.D.), the early Medieval Church was obliged to take into consideration the attitude inherited from past generations. The clergy of previous ages established the practice of gradually adopting and consecrating popular beliefs into some of the most important Church ceremonies, holy days, and even liturgical dances. Pope Gregory himself, cognizant of this history of assimilation, gave advice to the missionaries who were sent to convert the English heathen. He emphasized the necessity for compromise on unessential points: "Let the old temples be baptized to the new Church uses; let heathen festivals be retained, but let them be diverted from the worship of devils to that of the true God." [108]

This early Medieval Age is characterized by a struggle for unity. An example is Pope Gregory the Great's efforts to unify Eucharistic Liturgy. One problem that arose to test this unity was the Festival of Fools, with its singing, dancing and feasting in churches. The Festival of Fools was connected with festivals celebrated in ancient Rome at the end of December and in the beginning of January. After the Lombard invasion of Rome in 568 A.D., great festivals and organized shows and games are rarely mentioned as occurring in Rome itself. Dance continued to be performed but under the most unlikely of auspices—within the Church itself. People brought their dancing festivities into the churches. The Festival of Fools was "baptized," joined with the Christian Feast of the Circumcision or the Epiphany. [109]

The Councils of Toledo struggled with the unholy excesses that this festival seemed to bring forth. The Council of 589 A.D. simply tried to curtail excesses in dancing in their churches on the vigil of saints' days. But by 633 A.D., the Council again met and specifically forbade the Festival of Fools in churches with its singing, dancing, and feasting. Apparently the pagan element that was present, coupled with the undisciplined mass participation, made it difficult to accept the Festival of Fools into the Church's life.[110] Yet the Council of Toledo in 678 A.D. seemed to shift its opinion when it suggested that Archbishop Isidore of Seville compose and present a ritual that would be rich in sacred choreography. Following this suggestion, the dance ritual was eventually incorporated into the Mozarabic Rite and—amazingly—is still celebrated three times a year in the Cathedral of Seville.[111]

With the reign of Pepin, king of the Franks (741-768 A.D.), came the expansion of the sphere of influence of the somewhat stable Roman liturgy and the further unifying of the liturgy of the Church. Pepin requested that a copy of Gregory the Great's Roman Sacramentary be sent to him to serve as the basis for the liturgical reforms that he imposed upon his whole domain.[112] Restrictions on liturgical dance could also be expected to increase as this conscious use of authority

widened and deepened in Church and State.

Although dance was continually monitored, Pope Gregory IV (827-844 A.D.) showed his appreciation of dance by inaugurating the Children's Festival as a memorial to Pope Gregory the Great, who afterward became the patron of schools and students.[113] Much more was said about this Festival in consequent ages.

With the establishment of the Holy Roman Empire (800 A.D.), the Church's theological attitudes were affected. As the Mass became more and more removed from the people, the concept of Church as juridical institution began to outweigh the concept of Church as community. The accent on the mysterious in worship overrode the emphasis on celebration of praise to God. Concerning physical elements, the altar was pushed farther away from the people to make room for the seated clergy. The priest faced away from the people and prayed the Canon quietly. Controls abounded: the entrance procession was curtailed and loaves of unleavened bread were replaced by the "more practical" small white wafers received on the tongue. In short, the liturgy was becoming the special reserve of the clergy.[114] In desperation the laity adjusted to these changes by seeking out allegorical explanations of the Mass. Subjectivism eventually characterized the liturgy of the time.

Short plays were introduced into the liturgy to improve its intelligibility for the "simpliciores," as the laity were called. Before the end of the Early Middle Ages (1100 A.D.), playlets or tropes, the precursor of the Mystery Plays, began to make their way into the Eucharistic liturgy. A case in point is the "Quem Queritis" (ca. 970 A.D.), the earliest recorded playlet, written for Easter Mass. Anthony Schillaci wrote:

> It is interesting to recall . . . that popular preaching in the Middle Ages took on the features of theatrical events, and that the liturgy itself began to introduce drama as the means of reinforcing liturgical celebrations such as the Paschal Mystery.[115]

The playlet not only persisted in recognizable form up to the fifteenth century, but literally became "the bridge whereby medieval culture made the transition from ritual to representational drama."[116]

From the time of Gregory the Great to the onset of the Later Medieval Period, a change appeared to take place. The Church moved from an acceptance of dance as prayer to a more formal use of dance as a teaching device. Thus after Gregory, dance was still acceptable as a prayer form. But upon entering the Middle Ages the Chuch's attitude toward dance became more restrictive. Despite new edicts and legislation, the use of dance in its various Christian forms persisted into the next period.

CULTIC DANCE: LATER MEDIEVAL PERIOD

The Later Medieval Period (1100-1400 A.D.) was an age of dramatic expression. Oddly, the Church became the proponent of its own dramatic portrayals, having denounced the secular theatre as degenerate. The religious play became part of Mass itself and eventually began to take the form of mystery and miracle plays. In this same period, the use of dance became more and more widespread. But it is evident that the dancing within these religious dramatizations was mainly theatrical and not devotional.[117]

As the use of dance spread, so did its censorship. John Beleth, who lived in the twelfth century, recounted that among the kinds of dances in use at various Church festivals, one is the dancing festival of the choir boys on Innocents' Day—that is, the Children's Festival, inaugurated by Pope Gregory IV; another is the sub-deacon's dance on the feast of Circumcision or Epiphany—that is, the Feast of Fools.[118] Pierre de Corbeil, Archbishop of Sens, France (d.1222), added to the confusion by (most probably) composing the so-called Asses Song, sung at the church doors to begin the Festival of Fools.[119] This song was used for a few more centuries.

Both the Festival of Fools and the Festival of Children were accompanied at divine service (Liturgical Hours) and at Mass by dancing. Eventually during both festivals a "bishop" or "archbishop" or even "pope" were elected. All this was done in fun, ironically pretending to reverse the roles of laity with clergy in this age of hierarchical ascendancy in the Church.

The Dance of Death, "danse macabre," is certainly the most widely known of all the religious dances from the twelfth to the sixteenth century. There is much evidence that it was danced in Italy, Spain, France, Switzerland, Germany, and England. Its source is probably in the Medieval sermons of the mendicant orders on death. James Clark states that, "by the Dance of Death we understand literary or artistic representations of a procession or dance, in which both the living and the dead take part . . . The dance invariably expresses some allegorical, moral or satirical idea."[120] He goes on to state that the Dance of Death cannot be traced back to classical antiquity as would be supposed, but has its roots in the Middle Ages.

It began as a euphemistic treatment of "Death the brother of Sleep, approaching mortals gently . . ."[121] However, the later Medieval attitude was entirely different with the onset of the Black Death. Concerning death as treated in the later Medieval Dance of Death,

Its terrifying aspect was no longer softened or avoided, but deliberately emphasized (sic) . . . The solemn words 'Memento mori,' 'Remember that thou shalt die,' now acquire a new significance. To the ancients they meant 'Eat, drink, and be merry', to medieval people they were a call to repentance. In classical times the skeleton might seem a comic figure; in the Middle Ages it became inspiring or repellent.[122]

This transformation of the meaning of the Dance of Death was primarily due to the Black Death. This combination of bubonic plague and pneumonia raged through Europe and recurred in later years. By 1450 A.D., half of Europe had been destroyed by the Black Death. The people were preoccupied with death. There are even stories of dancing mania, an uncontrollable craze which spread all over Europe.[123]

The *death* of the Dance of Death was not to come until the seventeenth century. With the rise of new attitudes and tastes in the populace, it met its match. Once the worst of the Black Death had passed, the common people "no longer felt Death so imminent, commonplace, or close . . . Primarily because of a shift of interest away from things macabre, the Dances of Death went out of fashion in literature and art."[124]

Yet with all this happening, the Later Medieval Period gives evidence that the liturgical dance of joy and celebration was not dead. Eudes Rigaud, Archbishop of Rouen, records in his journal (1248-1275 A.D.) that in Villarceaux, France, cloistered nuns danced on the Feast of Holy Innocents and that priests danced in church on the Feast of Saint Nicholas.[125] Processions also began to be emphasized, complete with dancers. Pope Urban IV in 1264 A.D. created the Corpus Christi procession to celebrate the presence of Christ in the Eucharist. Though the idea took about fifty years to spread across Europe, the Portuguese Bishops in 1265 A.D. defined directions for this procession. It was to include all the people in the town and they were expected to dance and sing, using the more obvious religious symbols.[126]

Liturgically, participation in the Mass became even more restricted for the laity. Spectatorship was the hallmark of this period. Since Latin was no longer the language of the people, knowledge of the Mass was restricted to the educated and the clergy. Choirs took over all sung parts of Mass and left the rest of the laity to engage in private devotions during Mass. Allegorical explanations of Mass, such as that by Amalarius, Bishop of Metz (814 A.D.) became very popular.[127]

With the rise in papal control of all aspects of Christian life along with the excesses of the Dance of Death and the dancing mania, liturgical dance had even more difficulty surviving, but survive it did. At that time, the case for liturgical dance was still being supported by such persons as Andre Dias, a bishop in Portugal (ca.1367-1437 A.D.) who wrote poems in which he invited his monks to come and take holy communion "baylando e dancando."[128]

CULTIC DANCE: RENAISSANCE

The Renaissance (1400-1700 A.D.) followed. During this time, the dance in Christianity was going to fare well in processional celebrations, in the theatrical moral ballets, and in the interpretation of hymns and psalms in worship. During the fifteenth century the Children's Festival flourished more than the Festival of Fools[127] since the child-like qualities of the former seemed less threatening to Church authorities. But by 1528 A.D. even this Children's Festival was finding itself censured.[130]

Change and frequent upheaval characterized the Renaissance. The Great Western Schism was complete (1378-1417); books began to be printed (1455); the Protestant Reformation began (ca.1517-1529); the Council of Trent was convened (1545-1563); theater and spectacles were on the rise. All this complicated the Church's involvement in liturgical dance. Yet a core of supporters still could be found.

Cardinal Ximenes (1436-1517) restored the Mozarabic Rite at Toledo and Seville. This included the "seises" dances, which were performed seven times a year: on the feasts of Corpus Christi and the Immaculate Conception, during the octaves of the two and also during the three days of carnival. The "seises" were performed before the ark, which was placed on the altar. Six young boys dressed as angels or pages danced before the altar, accompanied by singing and the clicking of castanets.[131]

Typical of the confusion and lack of unanimity concerning the value of dance in the liturgy, Don Jayme de Palafox (1642-1701), Archbishop of Seville, attempted to suppress the "seises" in his archdiocese. As a consequence, the people of Seville collected enough money to send the choristers to Rome. In 1439 Pope Eugenius IV witnessed "los seises" and issued a Papal Bull authorizing these dancers to dance in the Seville cathedral. Dancers still perform today in this same cathedral, consistently testifying to the religious value found in liturgical dance.[132]

Soon after the Protestant Reformation began (1517-1529), the Council of Trent convened (1545-1563). Karl Young described the motivation of the Council Fathers:

> We may assume, then, that the removal of literary and dramatic interpolations from the Roman servicebooks legalized by the Council of Trent (1545-63) and the gradual disappearance of such intrusions from local uses, were inspired less by hostility to religious drama than by a fundamental determination to return all things to the purer and simpler liturgical tradition of the early Middle Ages.[133]

Again, the unity that was sought by the Church in liturgical and theological matters became even more important.

However altruistic the Council Fathers' motivation may have been, the results stifled creativity and growth within the liturgy. By 1570, Pius V completed the final editions of the Breviary and Missal. By systematizing and freezing liturgical rites into manuals and well-ordered texts, Trent made possible a simple, consistent form, able to be printed and distributed. But actually, the Age of Rubricism was beginning, perhaps unintentionally but effectively caste in cold, ecclesiastical stone until the beginning of the twentieth century.

Although the Council of Trent concluded with a lavish ball in which the Cardinals and Bishops participated,[134] and although Luther himself appreciated the place of dance in secular life,[135] the compound effect of Luther and Trent was the sounding of the eventual death-knell for liturgical dance, processions and most visual arts, leaving only the arts of printing, preaching, and music unscathed.

In the years following Trent, the "bergeratta"[136] dance was persistently used in the churches of Besancon, France, despite the synodal diocesan decrees of 1585 and 1601 that threatened severe penalties against those who kept this dance custom. In fact, this dance continued in the churches of that diocese until the year 1738.[137] In 1588 a defense of religious dancing was written by Thoinot Arbeau. He cited that "In the early church there was a custom which has endured until our time to sing the hymns of our faith while dancing, and this may still be observed in some places."[138] And in the classic work of 1682, Claude Francois Menestrier, a Jesuit priest from Paris, spoke of dance being used in Divine Office. He also pointed out that abuses had hurt the place of dance in liturgy.[139]

Backman, after listing an imposing number of proscriptions against religious dance, finally identified the cause of suppression of church dance:

> Some of these proscriptions afford important evidence as to the actual procedure of these church and churchyard dances. But how little did they affect popular custom! Dancing by the clergy was eventually stopped, except certain choristers' dances in Spain; but the Church was never able to suppress the popular church dances. It was only the Reformation, with its highly critical attitude towards traditional church customs and its fight against images and the worship of saints and pilgrimages, which ultimately succeeded in suppressing the church dance . . . One has the impression, however, that the Catholic Church was more or less resigned and contented itself with resisting strongly those dances which by their nature or by their obviously magic character and association with demonology dishonoured the Church.[140]

Then he wrote of how in Latin countries under Church control,

popular church dances flourished, freed from magical significance. He concluded by saying:

> As early as the days of the Church Fathers, the Councils were compelled to forbid and to issue warnings against these dances, but to no avail. From the eleventh century the proscriptions became more numerous, being most frequent between 1200 and 1500. . . . Our survey shows that the Christian religious dances continued from the end of the third century in unbroken succession until our own day. Not a single century is without its proscription.[141]

CULTIC DANCE: POST-RENAISSANCE

With the beginning of the Post-Renaissance Period (1700-1900), the Church, both Protestant and Catholic, firmly attempted to close the door on creative expression of dance in the liturgy. During the Renaissance, the increased frequency of the proscriptions against dance for Catholics was coupled with the increasing sense of mistrust of dance on the part of Protestant sects. This forced the dance back into the arms of society, more specifically court society, where dance found a home. By 1700, religious dancing either disappeared, survived in isolated places, changed into folk or court expressions, or remained nearly undiscernible, hidden just below the surface in the prescribed movements of the Mass itself.

Thus the history of dance had come full circle. From the period in which dance was accepted first by pagans and then by Jews and finally allowed by Christians, through the period of suspicion and then ever-increasing prohibitions, dance finally was forced out of its place in the liturgical celebrations of the Church. Society first relegated dance to use in its courtly ceremonies and then developed it into the sophistication of the ballet. Dance was given back totally to society, with few exceptions remaining of Church-related Christian dance.

CHAPTER 4

The Place of Movement in the Liturgical Prayer of Today

I t would be unfortunate to simply look back with nostalgia to the Jewish and Christian roots of liturgical dance and its persistence in worship and merely mourn all that has been lost. "We must," according to Michael Moynahan, "attempt to understand and distill the power and matrix of meaning that . . . Christian worshipers found in embodied prayer."[142]

HISTORICAL PERSPECTIVE

Through the centuries, the importance of movement in liturgical prayer has been persistent, struggling to evidence itself as a fitting instrument of religious meaning. Hugo Rahner was correct in stating that in almost every age, sacral dance "has been woven around the austere core of the liturgy."[143]

This has been true within the Judaeo-Christian tradition, although the history of dance in worship often left its clues only sparingly. In the early Church, the tradition seemed to have preserved the dance. Louis Bouyer described what he considered to be "the most ancient type of Christian church" by saying:

> The whole assembly, far from being a static mass of spectators, remains an organic gathering of worshippers, first centered on the Ark, for hearing and meditating on the scriptures, and finally going toward the East

all together, for the eucharistic prayer and the final communion. . . .
The 'action' remains a collective action . . . [with] full participation of
the women.[144]

In this context, Christians did attempt to give dance its sacral place and
justify it within the Christian Mystery. Unfortunately, this attempt was
shown principally, but not totally, in the form of ecclesiastical censures. However, it does seem reasonable and historically correct to
state that from the time of the Fathers of the Church up to almost
1300, it was not dancing *per se* which was originally censured, but
rather the low moral tone of the general festivities.[145]

With the Council of Wurzburg in 1298, dances were declared a
grevious sin. But dancing, and specifically religious dancing in the
churches during Eucharist and Divine Office, was not able to be
legislated out of existence that easily. The chronology of dance at the
end of this section affirms that. The rise in papal control and the
necessity of uniting and marshaling the forces of the Roman Church
against the effects of the Protestant Reformation dealt a crushing blow
to dance in the liturgy. The reverberations are still being felt today.
The question remains, what power and meaning can dance have for

the believers in the twentieth century and beyond?

Dom Gougaud, a French Benedictine, did considerable research at the beginning of the twentieth century on Christian liturgical dance and said that, concerning its formal acceptance into the liturgy:

> There is nothing to prove or even to render it probable that any kind of sacred dance was ever admitted into the liturgy of the Church either in antiquity or in the centuries that followed. In every age the dance was something that lay outside actual official worship. Having admitted this, we are certainly obligated to recognize, in so doing, that in all centuries, (dance) was customary in numerous churches in Christendom. . . . What was the attitude of the Church in the presence of these local customs? Often enough, she (the Church) condemned them by the agency of her scholars and councils. Occasionally she used tolerance, and this tolerance reaches even our own day in some customs of people who remember a time long past. But these (customs) are kept within bounds by ecclesiastical authority.[146]

Concerning the Church's basic attitude toward dance in the liturgy, Gougaud, said that generally ". . . the Church, without ever approving of (the dance) . . . being grafted onto her liturgy, seemed to have closed her eyes."[147]

PAPAL DOCUMENTS

Just a decade before Dom Gougaud published his findings, Pius X became the first pope to inaugurate any notable changes in the so-called liturgical Age of Rubricism, which had initially begun with the publication of the official Breviary and Missal by Pius V in 1570.

The motu proprio *Tra le Sollecitudini* (Nov. 22, 1903), published just a few months after Pius X ascended the Chair of Peter, aroused astonishment and was judged to be too daring and somewhat less than orthodox.[148] In it he stated that "active participation in the most sacred mysteries and in the public and solemn prayer of the Church" is the "first and indispensable source" of acquiring the Christian spirit.[149]

Other important signposts along the way of renewal gave reason to call this century the Age of Change and Restoration: Pius XI's *Divini Cultus* (1928) and several encyclicals of Pius XII: *Mystici Corporis* (1943), which formed the solid basis of theology for the later *Mediator Dei* (1947) and finally *Evangelii Praecones* (1951). Ritual changes were also introduced by Pius XII with the new liturgy for the Easter Vigil (1951) and for Holy Week (1955). The stage was being set. Theologians like Romano Guardini, already steeped in the history of liturgy, were exploring the wellspring of new, more biblical attitudes and their consequences for the liturgy. Shortly before World War II he wrote:

> The practice of the liturgy means that by the help of grace, under the guidance of the Church, we grow into living works of art before God, with no other aim or purpose than that of living and existing in His sight; it means fulfilling God's word and 'becoming as little children'; it means foregoing maturity with all its purposefulness, and confining oneself to play, as David did when he danced before the Ark. It may, of course, happen that those extremely clever people, who merely from being grown-up have lost all spiritual youth and spontaneity, will misunderstand this and jibe at it. David probably had to face the derision of Michal. . . . The soul . . . must learn to waste time for the sake of God, and to be prepared for the sacred game with sayings and thoughts and *gestures*, without always immediately asking 'why?' and 'wherefore?' [150]

During World War II he wrote that movement-prayer is a "form of speech by which the plain realities of the body say to God what its soul means and intends." [151]

VATICAN II AND THE CONSTITUTION ON THE SACRED LITURGY

With the publishing of the Constitution on the Liturgy, *Sacrosanctum Concilium*, the first official publication of the Second Vatican Council (Dec. 4, 1963), the Church "gave back to the human body its freedom to praise its creator in many different ways." [152] An examination of the document points out important shifts in certain theological and ritual areas, which will continue to be explored by the Church.

The first part of the opening chapter of the Constitution (articles 5-13) supports a new liturgical mentality in describing the theological nature of the liturgy and its importance in the life of the Church. [153] It is significant that the Council describes rather than defines active participation. Certainly it is not enough for the faithful to be physically present and to pray with a spirit of somewhat passive recollection (48). [154] It is necessary that ". . . their minds should be attuned to their voices" (11), [155] that they have an ". . . active participation in liturgy both internally and externally" (19), [156] and also that they participate ". . . by actions, gestures, and bodily attitudes" (30). [157] This "full, conscious and active participation" requested by the Council was not only "demanded by the very nature of the liturgy" but was also seen as the right and duty of all persons "by reason of their baptism" (14). [158] With the constant refrain of "active participation" being repeated, the Church was gradually ferreting out the deeper implications of the new attitudes expressed in the theology of Vatican II.

RECENT CHURCH DOCUMENTS

Almost a decade later the Bishops' Committee on the Liturgy published *Music in Catholic Worship,* a document that underscores the important function of gestures as assisting the assembly in meaningful involvement in the liturgy:

> We are celebrating when we involve ourselves meaningfully in the thoughts, words, songs, and gestures of the worshiping community— when everything we do is wholehearted and authentic for us — when we mean the words and want to do what is done.[159]

Also, concerning those who lead celebrations, they have as one of their tasks to lead the liturgical actions of the celebration well. "Faith grows when it is well expressed in celebration. Good celebrations foster and nourish faith." But the Bishops also mention rather forcefully that "Poor celebrations may weaken and destroy faith."[160] In other words, a liturgy that is highly articulate on the verbal level, but deficient in its gestures, could be a counter-faith sign. The call of the Church to foster participative, balanced, and integrated liturgy is getting louder.

By November 1, 1973, the Congregation of Divine Worship had published the *Directory For Masses With Children,* which was originally submitted about 1958 and had been reworked and resubmitted again and again. Finally, with its publication, Rome was officially recognizing what the principle of active participation and involvement means for children (and similarly for adults). The section entitled "Gestures and Actions" speaks of the nature of the liturgy as being "an activity of the entire man."[161] Not only are children to be involved by hearing words that make sense to them but also by the use of "gestures, posture, and action."[162] Both movement and silence have their place in Masses with children because "In their own way children are genuinely capable of reflection."[163] And lastly, concerning the use of visual elements, "The liturgy should never appear as something dry and merely intellectual."[164] It is *most* obvious that these basic principles for Masses with children also apply very well to Masses with adults: namely, liturgy must be an interesting activity involving the whole person and should be a blending of words, gestures and silence.

The most recent development in the Church's deepening appreciation of the importance of movement in liturgical prayer is *Environment and Art in Catholic Worship*, published in 1978 by the National Conference of Catholic Bishops. It contains a chapter entitled "The Arts and the Body Language of Liturgy" (55-62).[165] This chapter supports and sets standards not only for the gestures and bodily actions of the worshiping community but also for liturgical dance—bodily movement raised to the level of art. Concerning the worshiping community, the Bishops speak of the "tremendous impact" that the arts and bodily movement can create in the liturgy. Concerning the liturgical art of dance, *Environment and Art* states that: "Processions and interpretations through bodily movement (dance) can become meaningful parts of the liturgical celebration if done by truly competent persons in the manner that befits the total liturgical action" (59).[166] Carla Desola and Carolyn Deitering, both professionals in the liturgical art of dance, remind us that:

> . . . liturgical dancers should be well trained in the disciplines of their art as well as in liturgy . . . Perhaps the greatest obstacle to the acceptance of dance as a liturgical art (and the greatest objection to it by many who have witnessed it) is the fear of amateurism.[167]

THE NEED FOR CULTIC MOVEMENT

Even though the documents call attention to the importance and proper use of movement in liturgical prayer, the general experience of the North American segment of the Catholic Church, according to some liturgical scholars, is that our liturgy is "verbose,"[168] suffering from a "pervading ugliness and banality,"[169] "a solid barrage of words and concepts aimed primarily at the human intellect,"[170] and finally an experience of "halting gestures and raw stammering speech."[171] All these descriptions are not meant to describe contemporary worship as useless but merely to emphasize the fact that Vatican II's promoting of active participation by people in word and action (*Sacrosanctum Concilium*, 30) has only partially begun. Emphasis in this part of the world has centered mostly on the first part of this directive. But the much-needed enabling of assemblies and their ministers to pray comfortably, thus avoiding the self-conscious aspects of bodily movement and gesture, certainly needs much more exploration and implementation in the near future.

As in the early Church, some contemporary theologians and scholars view dance as essential to life. Hugo Rahner stated that "man in all ages . . . has always been a natural dancer . . . and has sought to express, in the sacral domain as in any other, whatever was really alive within his soul."[172] For Gerardus Van Der Leeuw, "The dance is not something in which we can participate or not, as we like. Whoever does not dance runs, races, waddles, limps—that is, he dances badly. We must all learn once more to dance."[173] Ladislas Orsy also described life as a dance with God:

> In a dance whose beauty transcends our desire and imagination God is the leading partner. We have to respond with our words, our eyes, our limbs, our whole body. This analogy is at home in all religions: man always incorporated sacred dancing into his worship.[174]

Lamenting the general state of the liturgy today, he stated:

> In our modern liturgy the responses in which our whole body takes part are reduced to bows and genuflections. There is room and need for some better movements in our sanctuaries to symbolize that God is our leading partner in a sacred dance that he initiated.[175]

Similarly, the United States Bishops' Committee on the Liturgy, conscious of the state of the liturgical celebrations in this country, issued a statement commemorating the fifteenth anniversary (1978) of the Constitution on the Liturgy. In it the bishops again remind their fellow Catholics that *"The arts cannot be divorced from authentic liturgical action."*[176]

Conclusions

It would be unfortunate if history were ignored. Even if good liturgical dance, formally speaking, may not be possible in many liturgical celebrations for valid liturgical and pastoral reasons, the need for forms of movement in our liturgical prayer must be examined. Attitudes that often resulted in the unwarranted suppresion of dance or other movement within the liturgy must be avoided. One of the most prevalent and dangerous attitudes seems to be a basic distrust of all things "affective" within liturgical celebrations. This tendency often results in the false dualism that supports an emphasis on the importance of soul over body, spiritual over physical, sacred over secular and urges persons to automatically choose trusted traditions over genuine, new developments, the fixed and solely rational, wordy prayer forms over the more spontaneous elements of celebration. The ideal of properly balanced, truly "affective" liturgy, as Ken Meltz mentions, is that it have the "capacity in ritual action to address the whole person, that is on a feeling as well as on a purely rational level."[177]

As the Bishops of the United States realize, dance does have the power to move our whole selves. It has the ability to change our hearts, our faith, and our theological perspective because it has the force of the Incarnation and Resurrection woven within and around it. Kister describes this:

> Because Christ expresses God to man in the flesh of the Incarnation, Christians know the supreme possibilities of bodily expression. Because Christ is risen, risen in the flesh, the graceful movements of expressive dance are a sign of that promised harmony and freedom from which all . . . yearn and toward which Christians strive in confident joy.[178]

The Bishops have accomplished a great deal in assessing and supporting the use and power of dance and all the arts in liturgical celebrations. Yet many persons refuse to see the place of dance within cultic worship. History has not ceased repeating itself and this is to be expected—but not necessarily welcomed. Realistically it is part of the ebb and flow the marks the history of the Barque of Peter. The documents of Vatican II, the *Directory For Masses With Children*, as well as *Environment and Art in Catholic Worship* stand intact as the most direct and affirming Church statements in the past five hundred years regarding the rightful place of dance in worship and the need for proper balance of word and action in the liturgy.

It is important to keep in mind that there are special qualities necessary if dance is to be used in the liturgy. It must be prayerful and faith-filled. Also it must not be simply "professional," the transfer of secular dance to religious surroundings. The Church is called to support and encourage the *new* Christian art of dance. It "must arise from the natural, God-given language of human movement, and be as limitless in its vocabulary as the God of whom it speaks is limitless!"[179] The creation of this type of dance, however, will paradoxically be both difficult and easy. It will be *difficult* in that these Christian dancers must be able to form their dance by getting in touch with their own feelings and faith rather than merely transposing forms used in theatrical or show dance. It will be *easy* because the material of their new-formed art is pure gift of love from God, the Prime Mover, the Leader of the Heavenly Dance.[180]

Liturgical dance, then, like the mysteries and unity of life it can communicate, actually belongs not to an age-long past but really ". . . to everyone who cares to feel and hear, see and touch, suffer and be moved . . . by God."[181] When Christians begin to open themselves to the beauty of liturgical prayer in the form of dance, then they can possibly "rediscover that bodily movement is not so much an instrument of enticement as an aid to profound human awareness and self-expression and a point of contact between man and the Spirit of God."[182] Perhaps it is true that, as Harvey Cox suggests, "in our own age a festive faith is now ready to celebrate in the flesh."[183]

In light of these reflections on the importance of movement in liturgical prayer from the Canaanites through Christianity to the present day, perhaps the question is no longer, "Should there be dancing in Christian worship?" There may be a new question emerging: "How and when can we (move or) dance in worship to express and experience the power of the liturgy most fully?"[184] The future importance of dance and the use of other gestures, postures and actions in the liturgy lies in the fact that they can encourage us to become more aware of the visual and tactile senses as vehicles of God's powerful presence in our daily lives. The present liturgical overemphasis on word-communication can, as the bishops remind us, stunt the faith-growth of our communities or even worse, weaken and destroy the faith now present.[185] The Church, true to the Kerygma, must gradually and wherever possible state boldly that the Resurrection of Jesus has beneficial consequences for us as full human beings and that the implications of that truth can and should affect the way we celebrate that life, the way "we live, and move, and exist" (Acts 17: 28).

Two vital kernals of truth about ourselves as human beings seem to emerge from the experience and matrix of meaning found in liturgical dance. One is that the "Incarnation, if it is anything more than a 'once-upon-a-time' story, means grace is carnal, healing comes through the flesh."[186] The other is that God is constantly inviting us to open ourselves to the loving, grace-filled touch of the "Leader of the Celestial Chorus." For too long have we said with our lips, "Let us praise the Lord with dancing" and have refused to dance. Let us finally welcome home the liturgical dance. Then perhaps Zephaniah's prophecy will be experienced as present and powerfully true in our day. We may even feel moved to join in the dance with God and the members of the human race as we hear:

> Zion, have no fear,
> do not let your hands fall limp.
> Yahweh your God is in your midst . . .
> He will exult with joy over you,
> he will renew you by his love;
> he will dance with shouts of joy for you
> as on a day of festival (3: 16-18).

Notes

[1]Hugo Rahner, *Man at Play*, trans. Brian Battershaw and Edward Quinn (New York: Herder and Herder, 1972), p. 67. An instance of this is given by quoting Plotinus: "for the true activity of life is that of the artist, such as the dancer in motion who is indeed the image and symbol thereof." (*Enneads*, III, 2, 16 [ed. von Harder, V, p. 45]).

[2]E. Louis Backman, *Religious Dances in the Christian Church and in Popular Medicine*, trans. E. Classen, (London: George Allen & Unwin Ltd., 1952), p. 1.

[3]*Man at Play*, p. 80.

[4]Among the authors who agree are: E. Louis Backman, *Religious Dances*, p. 1; Sigmund Mowinkel, *The Psalms in Israel's Worship*, trans. D. R. AP-Thomas, vol. 1, pp. 8-11; W. O. E. Oesterley, *The Sacred Dance; a study in Comparative Folklore* (Cambridge: Cambridge University Press, 1923), p. 53, 91 (note 2); Johs. Pedersen, *Israel; its Life and Culture*. vol. 3-4 (consecutive pagination), p. 436.

[5]These and all other scripture references, unless otherwise stated, will be taken from *The Jerusalem Bible*, ed. Alexander Jones (Garden City, N.Y.: Doubleday & Company, 1966).

[6]*Cosmos and History; The Myth of the Eternal Return*, trans. Willard R. Trask (New York: Harper Torchbooks, 1959), p. 28.

[7]*De Saltatione*, 7, trans. Leonard Wencis, Dissertation from Catholic University of America, March, 1969, (C. Jacobitz, II, p. 147 for Greek).

[8]Rahner, p. 71.

[9]John L. McKenzie, S.J. *The Two-Edged Sword; an Interpretation of the Old Testament* (Milwaukee: The Bruce Publishing Co., 1956), p. 46.

[10]Simon Dubnov, *History of the Jews*, trans. Moshe Spiegel, rev. ed. (New York: Thomas Yoseloff, 1967), vol. 1, p. 95.

[11]S. H. Hooke, ed., *Myth, Ritual and Kingship; Essays on the Theory and practice of Kingship in the Ancient Near East and In Israel* (Oxford, Clarendon Press, 1960), pp. 14-15.

[12]J. H. Eaton, "Dancing in the Old Testament," in J.G. Davies' *Worship and Dance* (University of Birmingham: N.P., 1975), p.4, emphasis is the author's.

[13]Georg Bertram, "παιζω," *Theological Dictionary of the New Testament*, ed. Gerhard Friedrich; ed. and trans. Geoffrey W. Bromiley (Grand Rapids, Mich.: Wm. B. Eerdmans Publ. Co., 1967), vol. 5, p. 627.

[14]J. H. Eaton in Davies' *Worship and Dance*, p. 5.

[15]W. O. E. Oesterley, *The Sacred Dance*, Op. cit.

[16]Oesterley, pp. 33-34.

[17]E. Louis Backman, *Religious Dances*, p. 10.

[18]Backman, p. 10.

[19]Roland E. Murphy, O. Carm. in "Psalms," in *The Jerome Biblical Commentary*

(Englewood Cliffs, N.J.: Prentice-Hall, Inc., 1968), vol. 1, art. 35, section 18, p. 575. Despite variances in more particular areas, most reknowned scripture scholars agree with the fact of the liturgical situation of the psalms:

Artur Weiser, *The Psalms; a Commentary* (Philadelphia: The Westminster Press, 1962), p. 23.

W. F. Albright, "The Role of the Canaanites in the History of Civilization," (Appendix I), in G. Ernest Wright, ed. *The Bible and the Ancient Near East* (Garden City, N.Y.: Doubleday & Company, Inc., 1961). p. 339.

Walter Harrelson, *From Fertility Cult to Worship* (Garden City, N.Y.: Doubleday & Co., 1969), p. 64.

S. H. Hooke, *Myth, Ritual and Kingship*, p. 8 and *The Origins of Early Semitic Ritual* (London: Oxford University Press, 1938), p. 55.

Hans-Joachim Kraus, *Worship in Israel; a Cultic History of the Old Testament*, trans. Geoffrey Buswell. (Richmond, Virginia: John Knox Press, 1965), p. 14.

Sigmund Mowinkel, *The Psalms in Israel's Worship*, vol. 1, p. 2 et passim.

W. O. E. Oesterley, *The Sacred Dance*, p. 55.

Norman Snaith, *Hymns of the Temple* (London: SCM Press Ltd., 1951), p. 7.

[20]Weiser, *The Psalms*, pp. 724-725, 729.

[21]Weiser, p. 487; authors who agree with his first point are:

Mitchell Dahood, S.J., *Psalms II; 51-100* (Garden City; N.Y.: Doubleday & Co., 1968), pp. 133-152

Sigmund Mowinkel, *The Psalms in Israel's Worship*, vol. 1, p. 125; vol. 2, p. 80. The second point is treated more fully below, notes 32-37 and 61-62.

[22]John J. Collins, "The Praises of Israel: Worship in the Old Testament," *Chicago Studies*, Vol. XVL, no. 1, (Spring, 1977), p. 104.

[23]Helene Lubienska de Lenval, *The Whole Man at Worship; The Actions of Man before God*, trans. Rachel Attwater (New York: Desclee Co., 1961), pp. 31-32.

[24]Eric Werner, *The Sacred Bridge*, p. 10 quotes the *Mishnah*, Sukkah. V. 1.

[25]Flavius Josephus, "Antiquities of the Jews," 8, 4, 1 in *Josephus: Complete Works*, trans. W. Whiston (Grand Rapids, Mich.: Kregel Publications, 1976), p. 176.

[26]Actually, the Israelites did not live in huts, but in *tents* during their days in the desert. Therefore the association is liturgical, *not* historical. (see John J. Castelot, S.S. "Religious Institutions of Israel," *The Jerome Biblical Commentary* (Englewood Cliffs, N.J.: Prentice-Hall, Inc, 1968), vol. 2, art. 76, sect. 148, p. 732.)

[27]Mitchell Dahood, S.J., *Psalms II; 51-100*, p. xvii prefers to speak of the Hebrew-Canaanite (linguistic) relationship as one of "influence" or "dependence" or in terms of "mutual elucidation".

[28]Roland de Vaux, O.P., *Ancient Israel; Its life and Institutions*, trans. John McHugh. (New York: McGraw-Hill Book Company, Inc., 1961), pp. 500-501; see also George W. MacRae, S.J., "The Meaning and Evolution of the Feast of Tabernacles," *The Catholic Biblical Quarterly*, XXII, (1960), p. 251.

[29]Oesterley, *Sacred Dance*, pp. 94 & 141.

[30]Mowinkel, *The Psalms in Israel's Worship*, vol. 1, p. 11 quotes *Mishna* Sukka IV, 9, and see also V, 5.

[31]Oesterley, *Sacred Dance*, p. 94.

[32]Johannes De Moor, *New Year with Canaanites and Israelites*, (Uitgegeven Door Uitgeversmaatschappij: J. H. Kok N.V. Kampen, 1972), par. #3.4, p. 29.

[33]George W. MacRae, S.J., "The Meaning and Evolution of the Feast of Tabernacles," *C.B.Q., Vol. XXII, (1960), p. 259.*

[34]MacRae, p. 259.

[35]S. G. F. Brandon, "The Myth and Ritual Position Critically Considered," in S. H. Hooke's *Myth, Ritual and Kingship*, pp. 285 & 287. This teleological interpretation of the past would exercise an even greater influence through Christianity (p. 287).

[36]Sigmund Mowinkel, *The Psalms*, vol. 1, p. 137, note 101.

[37]Sigmund Mowinkel, *He That Cometh*, trans. G. W. Anderson. (New York: Abington Press, 1954), p. 85.

[38]Walther Eichrodt, *Theology of the Old Testament*, trans. J.A. Baker (Philadephia: The Westminster Press, 1961), vol. 1, p. 318.

[39]Oesterley, *Sacred Dance*, p. 38; another instance is in 2 Samuel 6: 5a, where "David and all the House of Israel danced before Yahweh with all their might . . ."

[40]E. R. Dodds, *The Greeks and the Irrational* (Sather Classical Lectures, vol. XXV), (Berkeley: University of California Press, 1959), pp. 271-272.

[41]Joseph Bonsirven, S.J., *Palestinian Judaism in the Time of Christ*. trans. William Wolf (New York: McGraw-Hill Book Company, 1964), p. 260.

[42]*Ibid., p. 121.*

[43]K. Kohler, *Jewish Theology: Systematically and Historically Considered* (New York: KTAV Publishing House, Inc., 1968), p. 447.

[44]Bonsirven, pp. 120, 126 & 127.

[45]Charles Guignebert, *The Jewish World in the Time of Jesus* (New Hyde Park, New York: University Books, 1959), p. 74.

[46]Guignebert, p. 77.

[47]Louis Bouyer, *Liturgy and Architecture* (Notre Dame, Indiana: University of Notre Dame Press, 1967), pp. 9 & 10.

[48]Excellent scripture references to the Temple in the life of Jesus in Martin McNamara, M.S.C. "The Liturgical Assemblies and Religious Worship of the Early Christians," in *The Crisis of Liturgical Reform*, ed. Helmut Hucke (Concilium, vol. 42) (New York: Paulist Press, 1969), p. 22.

[49]W.O.E. Oesterley, *The Jewish Background of the Christian Liturgy* (Oxford: Clarendon Press, 1925), p. 85, quotes Prof. Bartlet.

[50]Bertram, p. 630.

[51]E. Louis Backman, *Religious Dances in the Christian Church*, p. 14.

[52]*Ibid.*, p. 13.

[53]Collins, *loc. cit.*

[54]"Liturgical Influences on the Formation of the Four Gospels," *C.B.Q.*, vol. XXI, pp. 35-36.

[55]This psalm was part of the music sung at the Feast of Tabernacles.

[56]*The Bible and the Liturgy*, (Liturgical Studies, Vol. 3), (Notre Dame, Indiana: University of Notre Dame Press, 1956), p. 341.

[57]Louis Bouyer, *The Fourth Gospel*, trans. Rev. Patrick Byrne, S.M. (Westminster, Maryland: The Newman Press, 1964), pp. 121-133.

George W. MacRae, S.J., "The Meaning and Evolution of the Feast of Tabernacles," in *C.B.Q.*, vol. XXII, pp. 275-276.

David Michael Stanley, S.J., "The Feast of Tents: Jesus' Self-Revelation," *Worship*, vol., 34 (Dec., 1959), pp. 20-27.

[58]Thierry Maertens, O.S.B., *A Feast in Honor of Yahweh*, trans. Mother Kathryn

Sullivan, R.S.C.J., (Notre Dame, Indiana: Fides Publishers, Inc., 1965), p. 239.

[59]For more on the Johannine conception of worship, see Oscar Cullmann, *Early Christian Worship*, trans. A. Stewart Todd and James B. Torrance, (Studies in Biblical Theology, No. 10) (London: SCM Press LTD., 1953), pp. 116-119.

[60]M. D. Goulder, *Midrash and Lection in Matthew: The Speaker's Lectures in Biblical Studies, 1969-71* (London: SPCK, 1974), p. 177.

[61]*Ibid.*, p. 178.

[62]*Ibid.*, pp. 364-382.

[63]Rudolf Bultmann, *Primitive Christianity; in its Contemporary Setting*, trans. Rev. R. H. Fuller, (New York: The World Publishing Company, 1956), pp. 175-177;

also S. H. Hooke, "Emergence of Christianity," in *Judaism and Christianity*, W.O.E. Oesterley, H. Loewe and Erwin I. J. Rosenthal, eds., vol. 1, (New York: KTAV Publishing House, Inc., 1969), p. 273.

[64]Josef A. Jungmann, S.J., *The Early Liturgy; to the Time of Gregory the Great*, trans. Francis A. Brunner, C.SS.R. (Liturgical Studies, vol. 6), (Notre Dame, Indiana: University of Notre Dame Press, 1959), p. 43.

[65]*Ibid.*, pp. 37-38.

[66]*Ibid.*, pp. 47-48.

[67]Hugo Rahner, "Meaning of the Dance," *Theology Digest*, XIV, (Autumn, 1966), p. 222.

[68]Book Third, Similitude Ninth, Chapter 11 in Alexander Roberts and James Donaldson, trans. *The Ante-Nicene Fathers: Translations of the Writings of the Fathers down to A.D. 325*, NS, vol. II, (New York; Charles Scribner's Sons. 1913), p. 47.

[69]Backman, p. 18.

[70]Roberts, *The Ante-Nicene Fathers*, p. 205 (Ch. 12).

[71]Backman, pp. 19-20 quoting Clement's "Address to the Heathens."

[72]Ambrose, "On Repentence, vol. 2, chapter 6" in Philip Schaff and Henry Wace, eds. *A Select Library of Nicene and Post-Nicene Fathers of the Christian Church*, NS, (Second series), vol. 10, p. 351.

[73]*Stromata*, see above; also in Lib. VII, Migne; P.G.9, col. 455. Paris, 1857.

[74]Jungmann, pp. 52 & 58.

[75]*Homiliae in Pascha*, 6 (PG. 59, 774D, f) as found in Hugo Rahner's *Man at Play*, p. 86.

[76]Hippolitus, In Canticum, 11 (G.C.S. I, i, pp. 347-348) as found in Hugo Rahner's *Man at Play*, p. 77. As Rahner observes in the footnote, these thoughts and expressions were borrowed by such great writers as Ambrose, Pseudo-Cassiodorus, Bede and Paterius.

[77]Quoted in Backman on p. 22, without primary references.

[78]F.X. Murphy, "Constantine I, the Great, Roman Emperor," in *New Catholic Encyclopedia*, (New York: McGraw-Hill Book Company, 1967), vol. 4, pp. 226-228.

[79]*Liturgy and Architecture*, pp. 40-44.

[80]*Ibid.*, p. 44.

[81]*Ibid.*, p. 48

[82]Rembert G. Weakland, "The 'Sacred' and the Liturgical Renewal," in *Worship*, 49: no. 9, p. 523.

[83]Book 10, ch. 9 of "The Church History of Eusebius" in Schaff and Wace, *Nicene and Post-Nicene Fathers*, (Second Series), vol. 1, p. 387.

[84]Backman, pp. 23-24.

[85]*Ibid.*, p. 155.

[86]*Ibid.*, p. 329.

[87]*Ibid.*, p. 24.

[88]Daniel A. Kister, "Dance and Theater in Christian Worship," *Worship*, vol. 45 (Dec., 1971), p. 591.

[89]*Comm. in Zach.*, *2.8* quoting 2 Samuel 6:22 as translated in J.G. Davies, ed., *Worship and Dance*, (Birmingham, Alabama: University of Birmigham, n.p., 1975), p. 55.

[90]Translated in Backman, p. 24.

[91]*Epist. ad I:2, translated in Backman, p. 25.*

[92]*Sermon on Drunkenness*, translated in Backman, *Ibid.*

[93]*Letters*, (58 in Benedictine enumeration but) 28, in Roy Joseph Deferrari, ed. *The Fathers of the Church: A New Translation*, vol. 26, trans. Sister Mary Melchior Beyenka, O.P., (New York: Fathers of the Church, Inc., 1954), p. 146.

[94]*Ibid.*, p. 145.

[95]See Note 72 above.

[96]"Concerning Virgins, book 3, ch. 5" in Philip Schaff and Henry Wace, eds. *Nicene and Post-Nicene Fathers*, (second series), vol. 10, p. 385.

[97]"Orationes, V" (Contra Julianum, 2) 35, quoted in Hugo Rahner's *Man at Play*, p. 77.

[98]Backman, p. 329.

[99]See note 76 above.

[100]"Homiliae in Psalmos, 6" quoted in Rahner, *Man at Play*, p. 89-90.

[101]*Ibid.*

[102]"Homily 48, 5" in Philip Schaff, ed. *A Select Library of the Nicene and Post-Nicene Fathers of the Christian Church*, (First Series), vol. 10, (New York: Charles Scribner's Sons, 1908), p. 299. Emphasis is added.

[103]"Sermo 311, 6 (In Natali Cypriani)" in Kister, p. 591.

[104]"Sermones, 311, 5-7" as quoted in Rahner, *Man at Play*, p. 81.

[105]F. Van Der Meer, *Augustine the Bishop; The Life and Work of a Father of the Church*, trans. Brian Battershaw and G. R. Lamb, (New York: Sheed and Ward, 1961), p. 515.

[106]"Sermones, 326, 1" quoted in Rahner, *Man at Play, Ibid.*

[107]"Sermones, 13, 4" in Roy Joseph Deferrari, ed., *The Fathers of the Church: A New Translation*, vol. 31, trans. Sister Mary Madeleine Meuller, O.S.F., (New York: Fathers of the Church, Inc., 1956), pp. 77-78.

[108]G. G. Coulton, *The Medieval Scene* (London: Cambridge University Press, 1967), p. 20.

[109]Backman, p. 51.

[110]Margaret Fisk Taylor, *A Time To Dance: Symbolic Movement in Worship* (Philadelphia: United Church Press, 1967), p. 102.

[111]Marilyn Daniels, *The Dance in Christianity: A History of Religious Dance Through The Ages* (New York: Paulist Press, 1981), p. 23.

[112]Archdale A. King, *Liturgies of the Past* (London: Longmans, Green & Co., Ltd., 1959), p. 102.

[113]Backman, p. 66.

[114]Ludwig Eisenhofer and Joseph Lechner, *The Liturgy of the Roman Rite* (New York: Herder and Herder, 1961), pp. 120-140 and 296.

[115]Anthony Schillaci, *Movies and Morals* (Notre Dame, Ind.,: Fides Books, 1968),

p. 114.

[116]O. B. Hardison, Jr., *Christian Rite and Christian Drama in the Middle Ages: Essays in the Origin & Early History of Modern Drama* (Baltimore: Johns Hopkins Press, 1965), p. 178.

[117]Taylor, p. 89.

[118]Backman, p. 51.

[119]*Ibid.*, pp. 53-54.

[120]James M. Clark, *The Dance of Death: in the Middle Ages and the Renaissance* (Glasgow: Jackson, Son & Co., 1950), p. 1.

[121]*Ibid.*, p. 2

[122]*Ibid.*

[123]Lincoln Kirstein, *The Book of the Dance* (New York: Garden City Publishing Co., Inc., 1942), p. 91.

[124]Henri Stegemeier, *The Dance of Death in Folksong, with an Introduction on the History of the Dance of Death* (Chicago: Univ. of Chicago Libraries, 1939), pp. 69 & 71.

[125]L. Gougaud, O.S.B., "La Danse Dans Les Eglises," *Revue D'Histoire Ecclesiastique*, 15 (1914), p. 232; translated by author.

[126]Jose Sasportes, "Feasts and Folias: The Dance in Portugal," *Dance Perspectives*, 42, (Summer, 1970), p. 14.

[127]Hardison, pp. 38-39.

[128]Sasportes, *loc. cit.*

[129]Backman, p. 65.

[130]*Ibid.*, p. 158.

[131]Taylor, pp. 83-84.

[132]Backman, p. 78 and Gougaud, pp. 244-245.

[133]Karl Young, *The Drama of the Medieval Church* (Oxford: Clarendon Press, 1933), vol. II, p. 419.

[134]Gaston Vuillier, *A History of Dancing: From the Earliest Ages to Our Own Times* (2nd ed.; New York: D. Appleton & Co., 1898), p. xi.

[135]Kirstein, p. 139.

[136]In the book of rites of the Church of Ste. Marie Magdaleine is described the Easter Day dance, the "bergeratta," which was performed in a serpentine manner in the cloisters or in the nave by the canons and choirboys at the conclusion of the sermon. (Taylor, pp. 110-111; Gougaud, p. 235). See also chronology following; 1582.

[137]Gougaud, p. 235.

[138]*Orchesography*, trans. Cyril Beaumont (London: Beaumont, 1925), p. 19.

[139]Claude Francois Menestrier, *Des Ballets Anciens et Moderne Selon Les Regles Du Theatre* (Paris: 1682; rpt. Geneva: Minkoff Reprint, 1972), pp. "e iij" (sic, preface) and 16.

[140]Backman, pp. 159-160.

[141]*Ibid.*, p. 161.

[142]Michael E. Moynahan, S.J., "Embodied Prayer in the Early Church," *Modern Liturgy*, 6, no. 5, (Aug., 1979), p. 26.

[143]Rahner, *Man at Play*, p. 80, as cited in footnote 3.

[144]*Liturgy and Architecture*. pp. 34-36.

[145]Kister, p. 489.

[146]Gougaud, p. 7.

[147]*Ibid.*, p. 147.

[148]William Barauna, O.F.M., "Active Participation," in *The Liturgy of Vatican II*, I, Engl. edit. ed. Jovian Lang, O.F.M. (Chicago: Franciscan Herald Press, 1966), p. 132.

[149]*Papal Teachings: The Liturgy*, Benedictine Monks of Solesmes, trans. Daughters of St. Paul (Boston: St. Paul Editions, 1962), p. 178.

[150]"Spirit of the Liturgy," in *The Church and the Catholic and the Spirit of the Liturgy*, trans. Ada Lane (New York: Sheed & Ward Inc., 1935), p. 183 (emphasis added).

[151]Romano Guardini, *Sacred Signs*, trans. Grace Branham (St. Louis, Mo.: Pio Decimo Press, 1956), p. 18.

[152]Boka di Mpasi Londi, "Freedom of Bodily Expression in African Liturgy," in *Symbol and Art in Worship*, ed. Luis Maldonado and David Power, (New York: Seabury Press, 1980), p. 53.

[153]"Constitution on the Sacred Liturgy," in *The Documents of Vatican II*, gen. ed. Walter M. Abbott, S.J. (New York: Guild Press, America Press, Association Press, 1966), pp. 137-144; all further references to the documents will be taken from this publication.

[154]*Ibid.*, p. 154.

[155]*Ibid.*, p. 143.

[156]*Ibid.*, p. 145.

[157]*Ibid.*, p. 148.

[158]*Ibid.*, p. 144.

[159]*Music in Catholic Worship*, (Washington D.C.: U.S.C.C., 1972, revised 1983).

[160]*Ibid.*, 6.

[161]*Directory for Masses with Children (Washington, D.C.: U.S.C.C., 1973).*

[162]*Ibid.*, 33.

[163]*Ibid.*, 37.

[164]*Ibid.*, 35.

[165]*Environment and Art in Catholic Worship* (Washington, D.C.: U.S.C.C, 1978).

[166]*Ibid.*, 59.

[167]"Dance: A Liturgical Art," *Pastoral Music*, vol. 5, no. 6, (Aug.-Sept., 1981), p. 20.

[168]Rembert G. Weakland, "The 'Sacred' and the Liturgical Renewal," *Worship*, 49, no. 9, p. 525.

[169]Myles Bourke, "The Future of the Liturgy: Some New Testament Guidelines," in *Toward Vatican III: The Work that Needs to be Done*, eds. David Tracy with Hans Kung and Johann B. Metz (New York: Seabury Press, 1978), p. 246, footnote 9.

[170]Ken Meltz, "A Program for Affective Liturgy," in *Aesthetic Dimensions of Religious Education*, eds. Gloria Durka and Joanmarie Smith (New York: Paulist Press, 1979), p. 89.

[171]Ralph Keifer, *Blessed and Broken: as Exploration of the Contemporary Experience of God in Eucharistic Celebration* (Wilmington, Delaware: Michael Glazier, Inc., 1982), p. 146.

[172]*Man at Play*, p. 82.

[173]*Sacred and Profane Beauty: The Holy in Art* (New York: Holt, Rinehart and Winston, 1963), p. 74.

[174]*The Lord of Confusion* (Denville, N.J.: Dimension Books, 1970), p. 107.

[175]*Ibid.*

[176]*Origins*, 8, no. 27, (Dec. 21, 1978), p. 425; the emphasis is in the text.

[177]Meltz, p. 86.

[178]Kister, p. 590.

[179]Desola and Deitering, p. 20.

[180]*Ibid.*

[181]Matthew Fox, O.P., *On Becoming a Musical Mystical Bear: Spirituality American Style* (New York: Paulist Press/Deus Books, 1976), p. 151.

[182]Kister, p. 593.

[183]*Feast of Fools; a Theological Essay on Festivity and Fantasy* (New York: Harper & Row, 1969), p. 53.

[184]Doug Adams, "Bringing the Whole Body to Liturgy," in *Modern Liturgy*, 4, no. 3 (March, 1977), p. 3.

[185]*Music in Catholic Worship*, 6.

[186]Sam Keen, *To a Dancing God* (New York: Harper & Row, 1970), p. 144.

Chronology of Liturgical Dance (300-1800) and the Events which shaped attitudes about Liturgical Dance.

Items in the left margin are events which were negative toward liturgical dance.

Items in the center margin are those events which evidence the use of liturgical dance or were positive toward liturgical dance.

Items in the far right margin are general events only indirectly affecting liturgical dance.

NOTE: Countries indicated in parentheses are listed according to present-day borders.

300-303 A.D. — Council of Alvira: ruled that women are not permitted to hold night watches in churches and churchyards; also, players, dancers and mimes were denied the Christian Sacrament.

313 - Edict of Milan: by Constantine the Great; mass conversions, Christianity publically accepted.

EARLY MIDDLE AGES: 500-1100

539 - Council of Toledo (Spain): condemned dancing in church processions in Spain and dancing in churches during vigil of saints' days.

554 - King Childebert (France) proscribed religious dances in his territories

which were held in churches on Easter, Christmas and other festivals. (Vuillier, p. 58; Davies, p. 16).

573-603- Council of Auxerres (France): forbade the public to dance in choir dances or in processions, or nuns to sing in them. (Gougaud, p.11)

589- Council of Toledo (Spain): tried to curtail exesses in dancing during the vigil of saint's days.

590-604- Pope Gregory the Great: simplified and fixed the text of the Canon and the readings for Mass.

633- Council of Toledo (Spain): forbade Festival of Fools in churches with its singing, dancing and feasting. (Daniels, p.22)

639- Council of Chalons-sur-Saone (France): forbade female choir dances in or near churches. (Gougaud, p.11)

> 678- Council of Toledo (Spain): suggested that Archbishop Isidore of Seville compose and present a ritual that would be rich in sacred choreography (see Mozarabic Rite in 1439); this ritual was presented in the seven churches of Toledo. (Daniels, p.22)

741-768- Pepin, the king of the Franks: established the Roman Liturgy (from Pope Gregory I) with additions from Gaul.

743- Council of Lessinas (in Hennehau, Germany): forbade laymen to dance in choir dances, and nuns to sing in churches.

> 800- Charlemagne: established the "Holy Roman Empire" and became emperor of the West.

> 814- Amalarius, Bishop of Metz (France): wrote and proposed a full-scale allegorical interpretation of the Mass; he was a prominent figure in the courts of Charlemagne and Louis the Pious (Hardison, p.37 & 78); his work was the standard of liturgical exegesis until the 1500's.

826- Council of Rome: forbade women to sing or perform choir dances. (Gougaud, p.12)

> 827-844- Pope Gregory IV inaugurated the Children's Festival as a memorial to Pope Gregory I, the eventual patron of schools and students. (Backman, p.66)

ca. 850-Pope Leo IV: ordered that women not dance or sing in churches and porches.

> ca. 900- Theophylactus, Patriarch of Constantino-

ple: introduced dance in churches or before altar on Christmas or Epiphany. (Backman, p. 59)

ca. 900- Regino, Abbot of Prium (Germany): forbade dancing in churchyards in death watches. (Backman, p.156)

ca. 970- "Quem Queritis": the earliest recorded playlet written for Easter celebrations, with miming indicated; very popular and seen as the bridge whereby medieval culture made the transition from ritual drama (in the Mass and the liturgy) to representational drama (mystery plays, dramas, etc.) (Hardison, pp. 178 & 288)

1000- Burchard of Worms (W. Germany): a question on confession: "Have you . . . danced as . . . the pagans do?" (Backman, p.156)

LATER MEDIEVAL PERIOD: 1100-1400

1136- Strasburg (E. Germany): in a church both the Feast of Fools and the Children's Festival were held.

ca. 1170- Balsamon, Patriarch of Antioch (Turkey): formulated proscriptions against dancing in churches of Constantinople, where they were performed on January 6th, the day of the Three Kings. (Backman, p.59)

1198- Bishop Eudes De Sully of Paris: forbade the Festival of Fools in French churches. (Backman, p.156)

ca. 1200: Cathedrals developed as symbolistic theaters for performance of Mass, parallel to the development of the cult of the Virgin Mary. (Kirstein, p. 342)

1200- Chartres (France): constructed the Cathedral with labyrinth in the floor, often used for dancing. (Daniels, p. 27)

1206- Synod of Cahors (France): threatened with excommunication those who danced inside or in front of churches.

1207- Pope Innocent III: issued a decree to Archbishops and Bishops principally in Poland, Mainz and Cologne, forbidding the Feast of Fools and the Children's Festival. (Backman, p.53)

1208- Bishop Cambius of Paris: repeated Bishop Eudes De Sully's proscription (1198) of the Feast of Fools in churches. (Gougaud, pp. 12 & 232)

1209- Council of Avignon (France): forbade dancing in churches in night watches. (Backman, p.157)

1212- Council of Paris: forbade the Festival of Fools in churches; this Festival now beginning to be called the Festival of Asses. (Backman, p. 51)

> 1215- Lateran Council: made yearly reception of the Eucharist obligatory.

1214- Synod of Rouen (France): forbade the Festival of Fools in churches.

> d. 1222- Pierre de Corbeil, Archbishop of Sens (France): composed the so-called Asses Song, sung at the church doors to begin the Festival of Fools (Asses). (Backman, pp. 53-54)

> ca. 1223- Francis of Assisi: obtained papal permission to install a stable and a crib, together with ox and ass in the church sanctuary. Mass was then celebrated around this scene. (Backman, p.63)

1227- Council of Trier (W. Germany): forbade three-step and ring dances in churches and churchyards.

1231- Council of Rouen (France): repeated Trier's proscriptions. (Gougaud, p.12)

> (1230-1296)- William Durandus, Bishop of Mende (France): described the *pilota* dance in his important handbook of the Mass. (Backman, p. 67)

> 1248-1275- (France): During these years, Eudes Rigaud, Archbishop of Rouen, recorded in his journal that in Villarceaux cloistered nuns danced on the Feast of the Holy Innocents; also he wrote that priests danced on the Feast of Saint Nicholas. (Gougaud, p.232)

1260- Synod of Cognac (France): forbade the Festival of Fools. (Gougaud, pp. 13 & 233)

> 1264- Pope Urban IV created the Corpus Christi procession to celebrate the presence of Christ in the Eucharist, though the idea did not spread across Europe until its confirmation by Pope Clement V in 1311 (Sasportes, p.14)

> 1265- (Portugal): Bishops defined directions for Corpus Christi procession; all the people of the town were to be present and to participate with dances and music as well as with the

more obvious religious symbols. (Sasportes, p.14)

(1265-1321)- Dante Alighieri wrote his "Divine Comedy" and began the stirrings of a renaissance.

1279- Council of Buda (Hungary): exhorted priests to prevent dancing in churches and churchyards.

1286- Council of Berry (France): restated Council of Buda (above).

1287- Council of Liege (Belgium): forbade dances in churches, porches and churchyards, especially at night watches and on the festivals of the saints.

1298- Synod of Tulle (France): repeated Liege (above).

1298- Council of Wurzburg (W. Germany): threatened heavy punishment and described dances at night watches and the saints' feasts as grievous sin. (Gougaud, p.13)

1309-1378- Avignon Papacy in France.

1308- Bishop of London: forbade ring dances in churchyards.

1318- Bishop of Lerida (Spain): forbade dance in churches and church yards.

1327- The church at Put (France): had a procession during Mass, called the Children's Festival. (Gougaud, p. 234)

1347-1373- Epidemic of the Black Death, a combination of bubonic plague and pneumonia, raged through Europe; the popularity of representations on the Dance of Death increased. (Taylor, p.97)

1350- Sacred dances given on Holy Thursday and Good Friday in a church in Florence (Italy).

1366- Synod of Prague (Czechoslovakia): forbade priests from singing in the Festival of Fools.

ca. 1367-1437- (Portugal): Andre Dias, Bishop in Portugal and Greece, wrote poems in which he invited his monks to come and take holy communion "baylando e dancando"; he also referred to the dance done in church during the first Mass celebrated by a newy ordained priest (forbidden in Portugal by 1477). (Sasportes, p.14)

1374- The greatest evidence of dance epidemics in Germany and Flanders. (Backman, pp. 331-334)

1377- Cathedral of Wurzburg (W. Germany): Cathedral Chapter condemned dancing at the Festival of Fools.

1378-1417- the Great Western Schism.

1389- Synod of Noyon (Naunet, France): inveighed against dancing in churches. (Backman, p.158)

THE RENAISSANCE: 1400-1700

1404- Synod of Langres (France): sought to proscribe the Festival of Fools. (Backman, p.158)

> 1411- Beauvais (France): the Asses Song sung at the doors of the church to begin the Feast of Asses; during Mass, as a part of this Festival, the priest would consume the "banquet" of coarse bread, blood pudding or blood sausage at the corner of the altar. (Backman, pp.53-55)

1429- Council of Paris: forbade priests to initiate dancing at the Festival of Fools.

> 1431- Henry VI: enters Paris; met by pageants, mimes and "mysteries" (i.e. mystery plays). (Kirstein, p.343).

1435- Council of Bale: tried to prohibit ring dances and plays in churches and churchyards, forbade the election of Fool's bishop and a Children's bishop. (Gougaud, p.13)

> (1436-1517) Cardinal Ximenes: restored the Mozarabic Rite (formed in 678) at Toledo and Seville, performed on the Feasts of Corpus Christi and the Immaculate Conception, during the octaves of the two, and the three days of carnival. He thus reinstated the "seises" dance of Seville. (Davies, p.19)
>
> 1439- Pope Eugenius IV in a Papal Bull authorized the "seises" (choir boy dances) for the Seville cathedral, an important part of the Corpus Christi processions in Medieval Spain. This happened when Don Jayme de Palafox, Archbishop of Seville, attempted to suppress them in his diocese. (Gougaud, pp.244-245)

1444- Theology Faculty in Paris: condemned Festival of Fools by sending a circular letter. (Backman, pp. 52 & 158)

1445- Council of Rouen (France): repeated statement of Theology Faculty of Paris.

> 1450- By this time half of Europe had been destroyed by the Black Death: this supported

the people's preoccupation with death and especially the Dance of Death and the dancing
mania. (Daniels, p.40)

1452- Pope Nicholas V or-
dered a theater to be
built. (Kirstein, p.343)
1453- in Besancon (France): the Dance of Death
was performed in the Church of Ste. Jean, after
the Franciscan community's Provincial Chapter. (Gougaud, p.231)

1455- Books began to be
printed.

1456- Council of Soissons (France): forbade ring dances in churches and
monasteries "as they disturb divine service and reverence for them."
(Gougaud, p.13)

1478- In a church in Hildesheim (W. Germany): a
round dance performed during Easter Mass.

1485-Council of Sens (France): repeated the statement of the Paris Faculty
of 1444.

1490- Sarum (England): maypole dance performed
in nave of the church. (Davies, p.17)
1490- Rheims Cathedral: Feast of Fools presented.
(Kirstein, p. 343)
1500- (Portugal): The King of Portugal and his
court danced the "Gloria" of the Mass inside
the church on Christmas morning. (Sasportes,
p.14)
1502-1534- (Portugal): During this time, Gil
Vicente wrote plays and gave shape to the various dramatic actions implicit in the popular,
religious and courtly festivities that preceded
him; he usually incorporated music and dances
in his plays as well as extensive masquerades,
thus anticipating the evolution of the ballet in
the following century in France. (Sasportess,
p.26)

ca. 1517-1529- Protestant Reformation began.
1518- Council of Strasburg (E. Germany): proscribed that music accompany
dance in church on account of the dancing epidemic; but the Council
specifically stated that this prohibition did not apply to the common
custom of the priest performing a sacral dance to special music at his first
Mass. (Gougaud, pp. 232-233, note 5)

1519- Emmanuel I (Portugal): prohibited dances in churches, but later other kings nullified his orders. (Sasportes, pp. 14, 17)

1525- Synod of Orleans (France): attempted to abolish all sorts of games, profane songs, plays and feasts in churches and churchyards.

1528- Council of Sens (France): condemned Festival of Fools and Children's Festival. (Backman, p.158)

1536- Council of Cologne (Germany): repeated Sens (1528) above.

1538- Parliament of Paris: condemned the "pilota" dance. (Backman, p.67)

1545-1563- Council of Trent (Italy): convened and began the Counter-Reformation; concluded with a ball in which the Cardinals and Bishops participated. (Vuillier, p.xi)

1546- Council of Rheims (France): forbade masquerades, plays, dances, and buying and selling in churches. (Davies, p.17)

1547- Parliament of Paris: prohibited the custom of music and dance at the first Mass of a new priest; condemned the custom of the priest dancing at this Mass. (Gougaud, pp.232-233, note 5)

1550- Synod of Chartres (France): reiterated Council of Sens (1528) above.

1551- Council of Narbonne (France): stated that "henceforth nobody will dare to dance in a holy temple or a churchyard during divine service." (Gougaud, p.13)

> 1555- Saint Teresa danced at Carmel in holy joy.

1560- Synod of Ancona (Italy): forbade three-step dances "by day or night in any church of the state or the city of Ancona." (Backman, pp.91 & 159)

1565- Synod of Compostella (Italy): forbade dances and plays during Mass, but the prohibition was soon withdrawn. (Backman, p.159)

1565- Council of Cambrai (France): prohibited Festival of Fools.

1566- Council of Toledo (Spain): described the Feast of Fools as an infamous abuse and forbade the election of so-called bishops. (Backman, p.159)

1566-1567- Council of Lyons (France): agreed with the Council of Toledo but also excommunicated priests and laity who led dances in churches or cemeteries. (Gougaud, p.14)

1568-1570- Pope Pius V: approved the final editions of the Breviary and Missal.

1570- Council of Mechlin (Belgium): sought to induce the *civil* authorities to prevent such dances as might seduce the congregation at Mass. (Backman, p.159)

1571- Synod of s'Hertogenbosch (Netherlands): reiterated the Synod of Mechlin (1570).

1575- Synod of Chartres (France): agree with Mechlin (1570) but prohibited the Festival of Fools.

> 1581- First ballet presented by Catherine de Medici at Fontainbleau. (Daniels, p.57)
>
> 1582- (France): in the book of rites of the church of Ste. Marie Magdaleine is described the Easter

> Day dance, the "bergeratta," which was performed in the churches of this diocese of Besacon, France; the dance was done in a serpentine manner in the cloisters or in the nave by the canons and choir boys at the conclusion of the sermon; despite the Synodal diocesan decrees of 1585 and 1601 that threatened severe penalties against those who kept up the dance custom, it continued in the churches of the diocese *until 1738.* (Gougaud, p.235)

1583- Council of Rheims (France): agreed with Council of Mechlin (1570).
1585- Council of Aix (France): agreed with Mechlin (1570).
1595- Synod of Angers (France): agreed with Synod of Chartres (1575).

> 1595- (France): in the Cathedral at Troyes, the Festival of Fools was held there for the last time. (Backman, p.64)
> 1609- Loreto (Italy): a church dance procession took place in celebration of canonization of Ignatius of Loyola.
> 1610- The religious dance, "ballet ambulatoire," performed to celebrate the canonization of Cardinal Charles Borromeo. (Taylor, p.113)
> 1615- (Portugal): The Jesuits had established fifteen colleges and used theater within the schools as a form of catechism and propaganda. (Sasportes, p.27)

1617- (Germany): Archbishop of Cologne forbade dances in church by bride and groom after the marriage ceremony and by the congregation at large. (Gougaud, p.14)

> 1619- (Portugal): The Jesuits organized a two-day street and theater spectacle for the reception of King Philip III of Spain and Portugal; the play had more than three hundred players and included dance and music. (Sasportes, pp. 27-28)
> 1634- A "moral ballet" composed to commemorate the birthday of the Cardinal of Savoy. (The word "ballet" implies a professional dance group for theatrical performance.) (Taylor, p.113)

1644- (Germany): Archbishop of Cologne forbade the Festival of Fools. (Backman, p.159)
1665- (Portugal): Public festivities of music and dance were controlled by law,

and a permit was needed to participate in them. (Sasportes, p.31)

1667- (France): Parliament of Paris forbade religious dances in general (Vuillier, p.58) and particularly the public dances of Jan. 1 and May 1, the torch dances of the first Sunday in Lent and those held around bonfires on the Vigil of St. John.

> 1682- Pere Menestrier, a Jesuit in Paris, published an interesting book on dancing. He described the abuses of his time concerning religious dancing and stated, "Our religious acts no longer consist of dancing, like those of the Jew and the heathen." (p.iv, erratic pagination).

POST-RENAISSANCE PERIOD: 1700-1900

1716- (Spain): Bishop of Lisbon renewed interdiction concerning plays and dances inside churches although the Corpus Christi procession remained untouched. (Sasportes, p.39)

> 1735- (Italy): The first opera house established. (Sasportes, p.32)

> 1749- (France): A Basque Bishop allowed male dancers and tambourine players to enter the church on Christmas Day and his permission was also extended to the festivals of the patron saints. (Davies, p.18)

1753- (Spain): Bishop of Barcelona forbade the eagle dance in churches. (Taylor, p.131)

> ca. 1765- (France): Near Brest, a Mr. Cambry noted that he witnessed a dance in the church and cemetery. (Gougaud, p.238)

1768- (Portugal): Marquis de Pombal expelled the Jesuits from Portugal.

1777- (Spain): A royal decree of Madrid sought to prevent all dancing on holy days in churches or churchyards or before images of the saints. (Kraus, p.57)

1780- (Spain): A royal decree stated that no dances could be performed in churches of the realm.

> 1794- (France): in the Cathedral of St. Lambert, in Liege, a choral dance was performed on the Tuesday after Pentecost. (Taylor, p.121)

(not many prohibitions after 1780's . . . .)

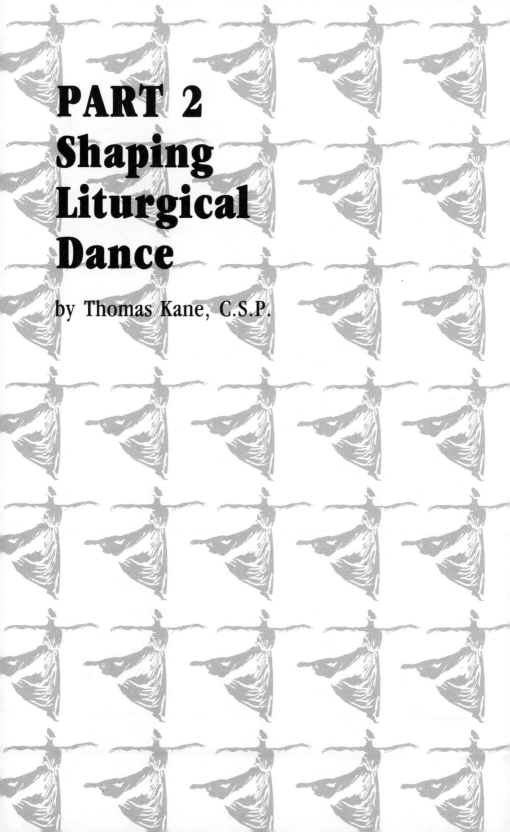

PART 2
Shaping
Liturgical
Dance

by Thomas Kane, C.S.P.

Introduction

Dance, the most universal of all the arts, is movement ordered by rhythm, time and space, expressing life and its deepest mysteries. Before speech, dance was the medium of communication of the human to the divine. History shows that dance has been significant to all aspects of life.

Throughout the world, various societies have performed dances for the planting and harvesting of crops, for rain and productivity, for rites of passage, for celebrating new life and commemorating the dead. The Hebrew scriptures record the frenzied dance of King David accompanying the ark into the city and the tambourine dance of Miriam after the Red Sea crossing.

In the Middle Ages, dance was often a significant aspect of religious and academic celebrations: there were Maypole dances at weddings and a ring dance for the conferring of doctoral degrees.[1] Today, dance is not only a part of our folk heritage, but is developing into a serious "performance" art. Modern dance and ballet are presented for a diversity of audiences across North America while folk dancing is taught in adult education classes and enjoyed at social dances and weddings. In the midst of a "dance explosion" religious groups are beginning to experience dance as a form of religious communication.

In the United States, the Shakers, the "Holy Rollers," and some Evangelical church groups have used and continue to use sacred dance or "the holy dance" in their worship. These dances might be a simple "circle dance" or ecstatic movement brought on by the spirit. Many mainline Christian churches are reclaiming sacred dance as part of their Western religious and cultural tradition by using dance in worship and instructing congregations about the art form.

At the same time, dance researchers are investigating the history of sacred dance and the role of dance throughout Christianity. As religious dance struggles to find its old-new identity, the effort is enriched by the growing interest and study of different types of dance in Western culture (especially folk dancing, ballet and modern dance) and the experimental work of contemporary liturgical dancers and choreographers.

CHAPTER 1

Sacred Dance and Liturgical Dance

S acred dance is *Prayer*. This is the primary feature which distinguishes sacred or religious dance from all other kinds of dance. A dancer may pray singly or in a group, using the body to commune with the divine or to acquire spiritual insight or special healing power. The Zar dances of Egypt, Shinto Temple dances, and contemporary liturgical dances are examples of this general type.[2] While some contemporary dances, like those of Martha Graham, may have a religious theme or relate a scriptural story, these dances are not sacred in the strict sense of the term.

Sacred dance takes different forms:

(1) Sacred dance might be *ecstatic* movement, which brings the dancer into a trance or altered state of consciousness. The revelers of Dionysios and the whirling dervishes achieve this state through their rhythmic movement.[3]

(2) Sacred dance may be *ritualistic*, where the entire ceremony is danced. The dance constitutes the ceremony, being the entire content of the ritual event. Cultural examples of this type abound from the Kachina dances of the Puebloan tribes to the Rejang Dance of Bali.[4]

(3) Sacred dance may also be *liturgical*, where the dance is a part of a larger ritual structure. Liturgical dance is not private activity, but a communal one, expressing religious sentiment within a liturgical framework. This type of sacred dance is not merely ornamental or decorative, but functions to deepen and focus the worship event.[5]

Today's interest in sacred dance is taking place alongside liturgical reform brought about by the Second Vatican Council. In dialogue with the modern world, the Church continues to revamp its worship, respecting the traditions of the past, yet recognizing the need for radical change in language, gesture, and art. Textual changes are only the start. The Liturgical Movement has sharpened our awareness for research in all aspects of the liturgy, especially the nonverbal, cultural, and aesthetic dimensions.

As a result, the traditional historical/theological approach is being augmented by ritual, ethnographic and phenomenological studies. Reform is more than translation as contemporary researchers seek an analysis of the communicative, artistic and performative aspects of the liturgy. The Vatican Council's *Constitution of the Church in the Modern World* stresses the relationship of art to human development:

> Let the Church also acknowledge new forms of art which are adapted to our age and in keeping with the characteristics of various nations and regions. Adjusted in their mode of expression and conformed to liturgical requirements, they may be introduced into the sanctuary when they raise the mind to God.[6]

The visual artist, the musician and composer, the dancer and choreographer, the architect and the poet must begin collaborating with church people so that new art forms may join the ancient forms to be not only *expressive* but *constitutive* of the Christian community of faith.

LITURGICAL DANCE

As a type of religious or sacred dance, liturgical dance includes body movement, attitude, and shaping and may involve an individual dancer, a group of dancers or the entire assembly. As ritual activity, liturgy has always employed different qualities of movement in its ceremonies, such as processing, bowing, kneeling and standing. In each case, liturgical dance is not mere performance, but connects with the prayer of the assembly. Liturgical dance does not interrupt or stop community prayer but continues and enriches it.

> The Liturgy of the Church has been rich in a tradition of ritual movement and gestures. These actions, subtly, yet really, contribute to an enviroment which can foster prayer or which can distract from prayer. When the gestures are done in common, they contribute to the unity of the worshipping assembly. Gestures which are broad and full in the visual and tactile sense, support the entire symbolic ritual.[7]

Within the Christian tradition, liturgical dance serves the worship of the church by drawing the community into the mysteries of worship, by revealing new dimensions of the scriptures, by witnessing to the beauty of God, and by eliciting a faith response from the community.[8] At the service of the community, liturgical dance bridges the visible and the invisible world of the spirit.

> Dance's gift in revelation is that by its unique, nonverbal interactions of spirit and body it can capture the nonverbal movements of the Holy Spirit in its interaction with people as it groans within them, moves through scripture and manifests itself in the mysteries of the liturgy. Dance can externalize these movements. Its makes them visible through the vehicle of the human body, drawing people into the mysteries through the use of basic, nonliteral materials. These include rhythms, dynamics, shapes, subtle and heightened creations of moods and feelings.[9]

The style, shape, and quality of movement for worship is in development. Not confined to a limited vocabulary of movement deemed "worshipful," liturgical dance is open to a variety of different dance traditions, such as modern dance, ballet, and yoga.

> This re-emergence of sacred dance will take forms that use aspects of folk dancing, square and popular dancing, ballet and modern dance and it will draw on the advances in psychological understanding for its depth and freedom and it will no doubt be affected by disciplines from other cultures . . .[10]

As movement styles are discovered, it is the task of present-day choreographers, dancers, and liturgists to evaluate new movements that are sacred, meaningful, and appropriate for church use. These forms may emerge from the indigenous culture or from the depths of a person's being. The movement is to express in a genuine way the faith of the assembly.

Liturgical dance presupposes a prayer life and a faith commitment or relationship to a spiritual force on the part of those involved. Because dance is a performance art, training and discipline for the art form are required of the solo dancer or group. Inexperienced dancers are to be discouraged from performing since they may detract from the prayer of the assembly. This kind of spontaneous movement is often confused with true folk art. Liturgical dance is too young and too vulnerable an art form to withstand such experimentation.

CHAPTER 2

Types of Liturgical Dance

A s dancers and liturgists continue to explore the dimensions of liturgical dance, a liturgical dance language is needed that respects both the liturgy and the dance. Dancers often use descriptive language to talk about the quality or shape of the movement. For example, it is quite common to hear of a "circle dance" or a reflective dance with sustained movement. Those involved in planning worship are often at a loss for words to describe the kind of movement or dance for a particular place or moment in the liturgy.

Because liturgical dance takes place within the structure of the worship service, dance types can be determined according to placement and function within the liturgy and by analyzing the source material (text or music) used for the dance. This decidedly functional approach provides a descriptive liturgical dance language. There are five types of liturgical dance: (1) *PROCESSION dance*; (2) *PROCLAMATION dance*; (3) *PRAYER dance*; (4) *MEDITATION dance*; and (5) *CELEBRATION dance*.

The examples of liturgical dance that follow were choreographed by Carla De Sola as a starting point and springboard for beginning liturgical dance groups. The suggested movements are direct and simple. Advanced groups can augment the basic movement.

PROCESSION DANCE

The procession dance is the purest form of religious dance. A latent awareness of the rhythms of life and the movement of a group attains a fixed form in processions.[11]

Processions and interpretations through bodily movement (dance) can

become meaningful parts of the liturgical celebration if done by truly competent persons in the manner that benefits the total liturgical action. A procession should move from one place to another with some purpose (not simply around the same space), and should normally include the congregation, sometimes with stops of stations for particular prayers, readings, or actions.[12]

Within the liturgy, there are four places which involve procession-like movement:

(1) The Entrance Procession gathers all those assembled into a liturgical community, sets the seasonal theme of the celebration and accompanies the ministers to the celebration space. The gathering is often achieved through the opening song, gathering song, or processional music. Simultaneously, the use of visuals, including banners, candles, area lighting, seasonal colors and movement can enhance the tone or theme. This might mean a riot of colors, a burst of trumpets and outwardly-directed movement for a joyous Easter or major feast day in contrast to a somber, reflective Lenten opening with sustained, inwardly-directed movement.

(2) The Gospel Procession highlights the proclamation of the good news of salvation from the Gospel book. The Alleluia or Gospel acclamation accompanies the procession to the ambo where the Gospel is proclaimed. All stand to sing it. This procession solemnizes the Gospel reading and may involve the Gospel reader, acolytes with candles and incense bearers. The Gospel book is ordinarily held high with sustained, graceful movement.

(3) The Gifts Procession highlights the preparation of the altar table and the bringing forth the elements of bread and wine from the community. Before the actual procession of the gifts, the altar table may be covered and arranged with candles and flowers. The aisle or aisles should be used to emphasize the movement of gifts from the gathered community to the table. On some occasions, other symbols can be effectively incorporated into the procession. However, the primary elements of bread and wine should not be obscured or eliminated.

(4) The Closing Procession signals the end of the liturgy and accompanies the ministers from the celebration space. Artistically, it is suggested that the opening and closing processions be of a similar quality or tone and involve the same ministers as the opening. In most cases, the opening and closing processions can be seen as parallel movements, directed to and from the celebration space.

Procession dance is primarily functional movement which accomplishes a particular task. All processions, whether danced or not, possess a dance-like quality.

PROCESSION DANCE

	Function	**Source Material**
Entrance or Gathering	gathers the community	sung or instrumental music
	opens the celebration	
	sets the theme	
	accompanies the minister to the celebration space	
Gospel	accompanies movement to the ambo	Alleluia/acclamation
	solemnizes the Gospel proclamation	
Gifts	accompanies the presentation of gifts of bread and wine by the assembly	sung or instrumental music
Closing	closes the celebration	sung or instrumental music
	accompanies the ministers from the celebration space	

O Come, O Come, Emmanuel

This is an entrance procession dance for the Advent season, incorporating the Advent wreath.

O Come, O Come, Emmanuel, and ransom captive Israel. On the words, "O Come, O Come . . ." the procession moves down the aisle, arms stretched in front, palms face upward. (Practice holding the arms out in such a way as to really feel them as an extension of the self seeking God.)

that mourns in lowly exile here. Leader with the wreath stops, and all the rest bow from the waist, lowering arms. (At this point in the third verse the sequence is changed. See later directions.)

until the son of God appear. All raise their bodies and lift up arms as before.

(Chorus) *Rejoice! Rejoice! Emmanuel.* The double line separates by everyone turning to face his or her partner and at the same time taking a big step backward, opening arms wide to the sides in a joyful manner. A pathway is thus formed down which the leader dances with the wreath. (It is easy to improvise with a wreath in one's hands. Show it off, turning from side to side in a spirit of delight.) The leader must be at the head of the line again in time for the next words.

shall come to thee, O Israel. The leader continues in front dancing, as the rest link right elbows with their partners, holding their free arms raised, and swing around one time in the center of the aisle. They end with their arms down by their sides, in original lines.

Repeat the entire sequence described so far, progressing toward the altar, while the assembly sings the second verse and chorus. By the third verse the leader places the wreath on a table and the double line separates to the left and right and encircles the table (leaving out the bowing). By the time of the third chorus, all are standing still facing the table.

(Chorus — third time) *Rejoice! Rejoice! Emmanuel.* On "Rejoice, rejoice," all take a step in toward the altar, hands held, arms lifting up. On "Emmanuel" all back away, lowering arms, dropping hands, and then lifting arms back out to the side.

shall come to thee, O Israel. All turn in place, arms lifted. Pause. The minister lights the first candle (on second week he or she lights the second candle, etc). and says a prayer for Advent. He or she then joins the groups and they all circle around the table, hands joined, as the next verse is sung, or simply hummed. The chorus movements are repeated as before (stepping toward the altar, arms raised, etc.) and all then slowly file off to their places in the assembly, as a final verse and chorus is sung.[13]

PROCLAMATION DANCE

Proclamation Dance forms the core of the Liturgy of the Word. It involves the proclamation of the Hebrew and Christian Scriptures and the Creed. The word instructs and nourishes the faithful in the continuing work of salvation while the Creed expresses the Christian faith as the basis for the community.

Dance drama or mime-dance (as it is sometimes called) may be the actual proclamation of the scriptures. At other times, the movement may augment the spoken text. In this way, reader and dancer jointly proclaim the message. The scriptures are so rich in stories, events and characters which lend themselves to a dramatic presentation. To dramatize the scriptures is to embody them, to make them part of the texture of our very being. As proclamation, movement can heighten, intensify or interpret the word in a new way.

Scriptures can be presented in such a way that our whole selves become engrossed in this learning about the kingdom. (How often is only our mind dimly engaged!) It is possible to see and feel and understand more of the depth and beauty of the scriptures when they are visualized for us in their presentations, "incarnated," as it were, through bodily participation. When our body and our sense are involved, our spirit becomes more involved, for we are a totality.[14]

On Sundays and feast days, there are generally three readings, one each from the Old Testament, epistles, and gospels. Proclamation dance may be (1) inspirational, heightening the proclamation in a dramatic way, (2) evangelical, witnessing to the good news, and (3) prophetic, revealing new dimensions of the Word or connecting its message to current events. (The psalms may be proclamation when used in the Liturgy of the Hours, but generally fall under the fourth category, meditation dance, when used as a response in the Eucharistic Liturgy.)

In addition to scriptural texts, it is possible on special occasions to include a special reading from a spiritual author, not included in the body of Scripture. A dance accompanying this reading would also be proclamation. For example, a dance to the writings of Teilhard de Chardin might be included in a Pentecost celebration.

PROCLAMATION DANCE

	Function	**Source Material**
Scriptural	to announce	Hebrew and Christian Scriptures
	to inspire/instruct	Scriptures
	to reveal	Creed
	to witness	
	to challenge	
Spiritual/historical	to inspire	thematic spiritual/ liturgical writing
	to witness	
	to challenge	

Quem Quaeritis?

This ancient play, *Quem Quaeritis?* (Whom do you seek?) was traditionally performed on Easter morning. It was the first piece of scripture to be dramatized for the liturgical service. This version was designed by Rick Hodsdon.

The three women, with bowed heads and gestures of mourning, weave their way down the aisle to the altar, saying to one another, "Who will roll the stone for us?" "Who will roll away the stone?"

At the altar, the angel suddenly appears. The women cry out and fall back, covering their faces. The angel says, "Don't be afraid. Whom are you looking for?"

The women rise and call, "Where is Jesus, the man who was crucified?"

The angel indicates the empty tomb: "He isn't here!" Raising arms slowly and majestically, the angel continues: "As he said, He has risen!" The angel gestures toward the assembly: "Now go and tell everybody!"

The women turn and call, "Peter! Andrew! James! John! Everyone! Hurry up! Come to the tomb!" They repeat this, running down the steps to the aisle. Then, dancing and spinning in joy, they cry out to people in each row such phrases as "Jesus is risen!" "The tomb! It's empty!" "Jesus is alive!" Hurry, come and see!" "Run and tell everyone!"

When they reach the back of the assembly, the disciples, and anyone else who wants to join in, run and skip and cartwheel forward, with ringing and jingling bells. Some call out: "Oh, Hallelujah! Jesus is risen!" Simultaneously, others cry: "Jesus is risen? I can't believe it!" Others, "Christ is alive! How can it be?" All converge at the altar, point out "the empty tomb" to each other, then are joined by the choir in leading the assembly in a favorite hymn of resurrection.[15]

PRAYER DANCE

Even though the nature of liturgical dance is prayer, there remains movement that expresses the prayer of the assembled community. Acclamation and invocation form two kinds of prayer dance. These prayers are usually addressed to God the Father and occasionally to Jesus Christ.

Acclamations are shouts of joy arising from the assembly as rousing assents of God's word and action. Acclamation dance includes the *Kyrie* (Lord, have mercy), *Sanctus* (Holy, holy), *Memorial Acclamation, Great Amen* and *Doxology* to the Lord's Prayer. These acclamations should be familiar to the worshipers, and liturgical music is readily available.

Invocations are prayers of praise and thanksgiving and include the *Gloria* (Glory to God) and the Lord's Prayer.

If prayer is the central core of life, then dance becomes prayer when we are expressing our relationship to God, to others, and to all the world of matter and spirit, through movement originating from our deepest

selves—this same central point of worship. The movements of dance-prayer start from our deep center, flow outward like rivulets into the stream of life, and impart life everywhere. So dance can be a part of prayer, just as stillness can be a part of movement and silence can be a part of music. There is one root; all the rest, movement or stillness, silence or sound, is its expression. The closer to the source, the purer the song.[16]

PRAYER DANCE

Function	Source Material
to acclaim	Kyrie (Lord, Have Mercy)
	Sanctus (Holy, Holy)
	Eucharistic Acclamation
	Great Amen
	Doxology to Lord's Prayer
to invoke	Lord's Prayer Blessing

The Lord's Prayer

It is possible for a dance to the Lord's Prayer to be simple enough for a whole assembly to learn. The text used here is the one prepared in 1975 by the International Consultation on English Texts.

> Opening position: Cross your arms in front of your body and take the hands of the person on either side of you. Still holding hands, bend over and remain in this position for a moment, with a sense of stillness and prayer.
>
> *Our Father in heaven, hallowed be your Name; your kingdom come, your will be done, on earth as in heaven:* Slowly raise your torso and at the same time lift your arms up in a smooth, continuous way, holding your neighbors' hands until you naturally let them go as your arms lift higher. (Avoid any pulling.) Uncross your arms (there will be a lovely moment of expansion when everyone does this at the same time) and hold them in an open, praising position, head and chest upraised.
>
> *Give us today our daily bread:* Lower your arms, bringing your hands together in a gesture of petition (palms face upward, arms stretched out in front of you about chest height).
>
> *Forgive us our sins:* Bow forward folding your arms to your chest with a sense of contrition.
>
> *As we forgive those who sin against us:* Come out of the bow and take the hands of the person on either side of you as a gesture of reconciliation. (Do not cross your arms this time.)
>
> *Save us from the time of trial:* Holding hands, all bow deeply.
>
> *And deliver us from evil:* Hold bow.
>
> *For the kingdom, the power, and the glory are yours, now and forever. Amen:* All raise arms and torsos, hands still joined. Rise to toes, and letting go of neighbors' hands, raise hands even higher in an exuberant Amen![17]

MEDITATION DANCE

Meditation Dance is reflective by nature, a response to a reading (psalm-meditation), a commentary on a group of thematic readings (homiletic), or a thanksgiving for a particular deed or event (post communion).

> Religious dance can be assumed to be the result of a personal, meditative experience of God; the movement's source comes from the heart's response, in an overflowing of gratitude or speech to God. In Christian terms, one could speak of Christ as the partner in an ever-new dance which is inspired by the Holy Spirit and offered to the Father.[18]

The principal use of the psalm-dance is a meditative response to the first reading of the liturgy. The text of the psalm is usually poetic, providing insight into the reading and thematically related to it. A psalm-dance may also be used as a contemplative element after communion. In both instances, the psalm-dance may incorporate communal gesture along with solo or group movement.

The use of a meditation dance may also take the form of a homily or sermon. This dance may inspire, challenge, or proclaim the message of salvation in a special way. It is possible to have a solo

dance or a dance used in conjunction with a spoken sermon. The dance is to draw the community into reflecting on the impact of the message on their daily lives.

Meditation dance is most popularly associated with the quiet time after communion. As the ritual draws to a close, this contemplative time can reinforce the theme of the celebration, draw the community together in a spirit of thanksgiving or help provide insight into the meaning of the celebration.

MEDITATION DANCE

	Function	Source Material
Psalm-dance	to respond meditatively to the first reading	psalm
	to draw the community into a reflective spirit	
homiletic	to share with the community the implications and impact of the good news (prophetic)	scripture texts
	to witness to the truth of the good news (evangelical)	
after communion	to reinforce the theme of the celebration	sung or instrumental music
	to inspire	
	to give thanks (communal)	

Psalm 36

This is a psalm prayer in movement, to be done in pairs by any even number of persons.

> *How precious is thy steadfast love, O God!* Take partners and spread out. One member of each pair begins by kneeling, or sitting back on his or her heels, body bent over; the other begins by standing, facing the partner. Hold this position while the first line is slowly sung or read. Then in response, the person kneeling raises his or her back and lifts up his or her hands, palms upward, as the standing person (a "God figure" of love) bends forward and lowers the hands, palms downward, till they meet the upraised hands of the partner. This is done very slowly, so that the meeting of the hands becomes a meaningful moment.

> *The children of men/women take refuge in the shadow of thy wings.* While the line is sung or read, the lower person in each set rises to his or her knees and each couple then slowly embraces, folding arms around

one another, each in his or her own way.

They feast on the abundance of thy house. The "God figure" helps the kneeling person to rise, then grasps with the right hand the partner's left hand and steps backward in a small circle, as the partner walks forward. The "God figure" leads the other gently around, gestures with the free hand as if showing the "house" — the river of delights. Think of it as a thanksgiving in movement for God's bounty.

And thou givest them drink from the river of thy delights. The "God figure" bends down as if scooping imaginary water and rising, passes it to the partner who with cupped hands and swaying body accepts it in a variety of ways (as of drinking deeply, or bathing in a fountain, etc.). This passing and receiving can be done a number of times.

For with thee is the fountain of delight. Both persons gradually stop the gesture, and come to a standing position facing each other, a few feet apart. Both persons place their hands with palms facing inward, a few inches in front of their own face.

In thy light do we see light. All slowly separate their hands as if parting a curtain and look at their partner face to face, receiving "light" from one another. This position is held for a few seconds.

Note: This is simply an outline for a movement meditation. Each couple must make it their own. If possible, go over the text beforehand and have someone lead some movement warm-ups.[19]

CELEBRATION DANCE

Celebration dance may be considered liturgical dance, although it is not formally connected to the ritual structure. More akin to the prelude and postlude of a liturgical service, celebration dance sets the tone for a festive gathering or brings it to a festive close. These dances tend to involve the entire assembly either in a simple gesture or actual movement. Circle dances that encompass the entire space at the end of a liturgy exemplify this type.

CELEBRATION DANCE

Function	Source Material
to prepare the assembly for festivity	sung or instrumental music
to conclude the celebration in a special way	

A Gift to Be Simple

If one thinks of religious dance in America, the Shakers always come to mind, for they were a religious sect for whom dance was an integral aspect of worship. Founded in England, they came to the East and Midwest in the late eighteenth century and created many songs and dances to express their delight in God.

A Gift to Be Simple is one of the best known examples of their dances and songs. This dance was taught to Carla DeSola by a person living in the vicinity of a Shaker Village.[20]

Opening formation: a circle, all facing center.

'Tis the gift to be simple, 'tis the gift to be free: All take four steps toward

the center, beginning with the right foot (r,1,r,1). Hands are held in front of the body; about waist height, palms facing upward. Initiated by a gentle wrist movement, the hands pulse upward and downward. (This up-and-down movement with upturned hands was thought of as a gesture to receive grace.)

'Tis the gift to come down where we ought to be: All take four steps back to place (r,1,r,1). The palms face downward as you walk backward, and shake in a small down-and-up direction. This movement, with turned down palms, was used to signify shaking out bad influences, or "all that is carnal." (There is a Shaker song with the words, "Come life, Shaker life, come life eternal, shake, shake out of me all that is carnal.")

And when we find ourselves in the place just right, we will be in the valley of love and delight: Repeat the above pattern; four steps into the center and four steps back to place.

When true simplicity is gained: Bring hands to prayer position (palms together, fingertips pointing upward). Step to the right with the right foot and bring the left foot to meet the right, bending both knees. Reverse to the left on the words, "simplicity is gained."

To bow and to bend we shall not be ashamed: Repeat the above pattern (stepping and bending to the right and then to the left).

To turn, turn will be our delight: Keeping hands in the same prayer position, turn in place by making a small circle to the right (step r,1,r,1). End facing the center.

Till by turning, turning we come round right: Reverse. (Make a small circle to the left, stepping 1,r,1,r).[19]

The following outlines show the diversity of liturgical dance types in relation to the order of the Eucharistic service:

RELATIONSHIP OF DANCE TYPES TO ELEMENTS OF EUCHARISTIC CELEBRATION

The Eucharistic Liturgy	Liturgical Dance Types
Prelude	(5) Celebration

INTRODUCTORY RITES:	
Opening Song/Music	(1) Procession
Penitential Rite *(Kyrie)*	(3) Prayer
Glory to God *(Gloria)*	(3) Prayer

LITURGY OF THE WORD:	
First Reading	(2) Proclamation
Psalm Response	(4) Meditation
Second Reading	(2) Proclamation
Alleluia	(1) Procession
Gospel	(2) Proclamation
Homily	(4) Meditation
The Creed *(Credo)*	(2) Proclamation

LITURGY OF THE EUCHARIST:	
Preparation of Bread and Wine	(1) Procession
Holy, Holy *(Sanctus)*	(3) Prayer
Acclamation	(3) Prayer
Amen	(3) Prayer
The Lord's Prayer	(3) Prayer
Communion	(4) Meditation

CLOSING RITE:	
Blessing/Dismissal	(3) Prayer
Closing Song/Music	(1) Procession
Postlude	(5) Celebration

Conclusions

(1) Liturgical dance is largely determined by the ritual structure in which it is performed.

(2) Liturgical dance must clearly be prayer and not performance. It is intended to involve all the participants in the ritual action. In ritual, there are no spectators; all participate.

(3) Liturgical dance includes solo and group dances and may include assembly dance or gesture.

(4) Liturgical dance is communal, drawing the community together.

(5) Liturgical dance is inspirational, uplifting the spirit to God.

(6) Liturgical dance is evangelical, witnessing to the message of salvation.

(7) Liturgical dance is prophetic, challenging the participants to live the message.

Notes

[1]Gerardus van der Leeuw, *Sacred and Profane Beauty: The Holy in Art* (Nashville: Abingdon Press, 1963) p. 32.

[2]Judith Lynne Hanna, *To Dance is Human* (Austin, Texas: University of Texas, 1979) pp. 106-110.

[3]Jamake Highwater, *Dance: Rituals of Experience* (New York: A and W Publishing Co., 1978) pp. 41-43 and Annemarie Schimmel, "Rituals of Rebirth," *Parabola*, Volume 4, No. 2, pp. 89-90.

[4]Highwater, *op. cit.,* pp. 17-41.

[5]Carla DeSola, *The Spirit Moves* (Washington, D.C.: The Liturgical Conference, 1977) p. 147.

[6]"Pastoral Constitution of the Church in the Modern World," paragraph 62, *The Documents of Vatican II*, ed. by Walter M. Abbott, S.J. (New York: The America Press, 1966).

[7]*Art and Environment in Catholic Worship*, paragraph 56, (Washington, D.C.: U.S.C.C., 1978).

[8]DeSola, *op. cit.,* p. 147.

[9]*Ibid*, p. 147.

[10]*Ibid*, p. 3.

[11]Van der Leeuw, *op. cit.,* p. 39.

[12]*Art and Environment In Catholic Worship,* paragraph 58.

[13]DeSola, *op. cit.,* pp. 40-41.

[14]*Ibid*, p. 95.

[15]*Ibid*, pp. 91-92.

[16]*Ibid*, p. 2.

[17]*Ibid*, pp. 30-31.

[17]Carla DeSola and Arthur Daton, "Awakening the Right Lobe through Dance," *Aesthetic Dimensions of Religious Education*, ed. by Gloria Durka and Joanmarie Smith (New York: Paulist Press, 1979) p. 73.

[19]DeSola, *The Spirit Moves*, pp. 98-99.

[20]See Edward Andrews, *The Gift to be Simple: Songs, Dances and Rituals of the American Shakers* (New York: Dover Publications, 1962).

[21]DeSola, *The Spirit Moves*, pp. 120-121.

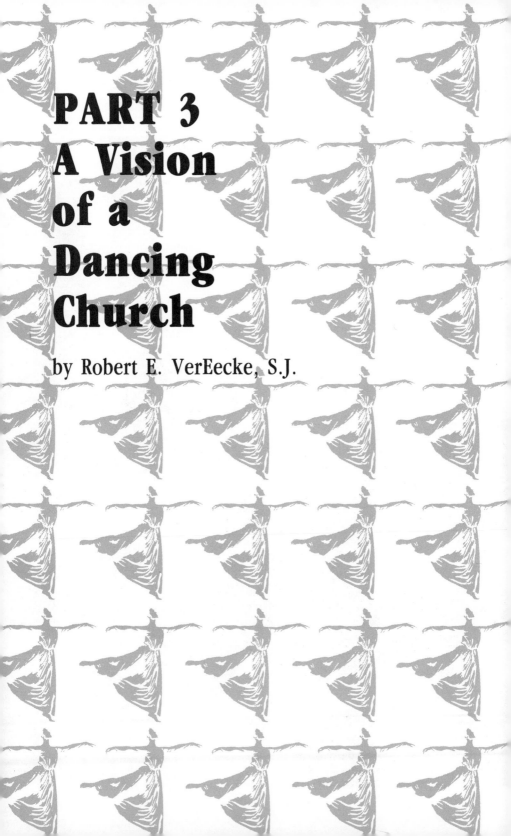

PART 3
A Vision
of a
Dancing
Church

by Robert E. VerEecke, S.J.

Introduction

It is Easter morning. As the first rays of the sun begin to penetrate the darkness, a people gathers. In a place made sacred by their presence, with windows on all sides revealing the panoramic beauty of nature and cities around them, a people begins to move in procession. As the gentle pulses of Pachelbel's *Canon* break the silence of the dawn, a people begins to move in rhythmic measure . . . from all sides converging toward a central point. With flowers in hand they take three steps forward and two back, turning to face the person behind, reaching toward, drawing into, sharing the gift . . . three steps backward and two forward, the procession continues. As the light fills the space, announcing the dawn of new life, a people dances, hands joined together . . . concentric circles . . . weaving the vine, the familiar pattern of a joyful people. As this people dances, one in the center holding the Easter candle high, turning so that all may see, blesses the water with this light so that all may bless themselves with the new living waters. As a waiting, watchful people waits for the dawn of an Easter day, they assemble to celebrate in a special way. It is the dawn of a dancing Church with the Lord of Life, dancing in the midst of God's people.

This vision of a dancing Church may seem far fetched to some, far out to others and far away to those who have lost hope in a vibrant, living Church. To a trained dancer, choreographer and ordained Roman Catholic priest, the vision described is not far fetched, far out or far away. It is a vision firmly rooted in Creation-Incarnation theology, supported by scripture and liturgical praxis and is very much an experience of the contemporary church. As a "dancing priest" I have been invited in the context of my faith experience to explore, create and reflect on the visions and realities of a dancing Church. Despite reservations, skepticism and sometimes antagonism, I have come to believe in this dancing people of God and myself as one whose task it is to help form this people.

One of the major oppositions to this reality of a people of God expressing their faith in creative, artistic ways is the attitude of some church officials that "creativity bewilders the faithful" (from the forward of a 1980 Roman document concerning the Eucharist). The statement captures a prevalent attitude in the church through the ages. Creativity, imagination, and artistic expression are dangerous dynamics of the human spirit. Care must be taken that they are used within limits and with restraint. Artists themselves have always been suspect and considered to be less than respectable, stable or "solid." The irony of this position, however, is that the arts have nurtured and sustained the faithful throughout the ages. It is not so much the doctrines and creeds in themselves that have inspired, but more the imagination of artists out of whose faith has sprung life-giving images that nourish the faith experience of others. It is the image of the Michaelangelo "Pieta" that is etched in the human heart as an affirmation of the humanity of Jesus. [It is] the myriad artistic expressions of the cross and passion which open up for people the extraordinary love of God for humankind in Jesus Christ. It is the poetry of Gerard Manley Hopkins that explores and uncovers the mystery of the Incarnation as it is enfleshed in the life of one human being. It is the overpowering beauty of the *Bach B Minor Mass* that invites the listener to an experience of the power and mystery of God. It is the cathedrals, the paintings, the music, the drama, the sculpture, the poetry, these "works of human hands," which have inspired persons through the centuries. The arts have enabled the human spirit to soar to union with God, to touch, even for a moment, the ecstasy and beauty of the Creator, the first Artist.

My own experience of the power of the arts to unfold and communicate the mystery of God's self-revelation through the human is rooted in my experience as a dancer. It is through the dance that the most stunning moments of union with God have been mine. Three "peak" experiences can only indicate the level and intensity of those "moments of union" as they were enfleshed in the struggle of the human body to bring to expression the yearning of the human spirit for meaning in the context of life's mystery. The first happened during a performance of Jose Limon's choreography for Kodaly's *Missa Brevis*. The setting is a war-torn church in Hungary. The dancers dance the section of the Mass against this background of tragedy and wasted life. As the "Sanctus" section of the *Missa* was danced, a sense of the fragility of human movement trying to communicate the mystery of human life overwhelmed me. It was as if the very heart of God was being disclosed through the experience of human gesture and movement. There in the middle of the theater in the darkness, I experienced the tears that come from recognition of the presence of God in the midst of the human struggle. Although this was no "Church," the realization was a deeply religious one, a moment of "awe-ful" realization of God's human dwelling place.

The second comes from a personal experience of "movement-prayer." In Bernstein's *Mass*, the opening song is "A Simple Song."

The melody, lyrics and rhythms combined beautifully to express an experience of God as "the simplest of all." It was my desire to try to capture this idea, emotion, and experience using movement. In the process of creating this dance, inspired by this "Simple Song," I found that the movement itself led to prayer, a dialogue through the body with its creator. Although the music touched and inspired me to move, it was ultimately the movement that became my vehicle of communication with God. There are a few movements in particular that enabled me to feel an almost perfect integration of body and spirit, expressing a profound belief in a complex but simple God.

In the introductory section there are two simple gestures that relate to the musical and verbal expression, "For God is the simplest of all." The movement range is formed by placing the right hand in a crossed position over the left, on one musical phrase, then stretching the right arm to full extension upward on a diagonal line, torso leaning sideways as the left arm extends the line downward; an expressive line between heaven and earth with the human heart at the center. Later in the song, there is the image "The sun shall not smite me by day, nor the moon by night." In a similar body position as just described, the palm of the right hand shades the body, as a protective, caring gesture. This pose, momentarily held, develops into a tremulous quivering of the whole body as it explodes with an energy of confidence and trust into a strong "turn in attitude." The final movement is a technically complex movement that can reveal the precarious balance between the human desire for surrender to God and the simultaneous fear of letting go. Because the movement is so complex it can mean many things. Balanced only on the ball of the right foot, the dancer places his head on the altar, resting it for a moment as he extends the left leg into the air in arabesque penché. As I danced this technically difficult movement, the emotion I felt within was quite simple. I wanted to take the risk, to let go of everything and be one in love with my God. This experience of moving prayer gave me a sense of power, of beauty, of a dynamic spirit of God dwelling in me and able to be expressed through my flesh. It was an experience rooted in the finite limitation of human grace but open to the full expression of divine graciousness, manifested through the grace of the human body and spirit in motion or in stillness.

The third "peak" experience came in the context of a "dance retreat." The purpose of these dance retreat weekends is to bring together people of all ages and backgrounds to explore individual and communal movement prayer. At one point in the first weekend retreat, as the group 'embodied' their prayer as one, I was incredibly moved with a sense of God's presence in this moving community. As I saw them move and pray together I had a tangible sense of God's spirit in human shape and form. It was as if the theological affirmation, "one

Body, one Spirit'' had taken on a clear and recognizable life.

These three experiences are particularly significant because they represent the three different facets of dance as religious experience that have nurtured my journey as an artist in the Church. Each has offered avenues of bringing to life a vision of a dancing Church. Dance as performance, as liturgical prayer and as communal expression of faith has opened up for me new ways of exploring the age-old stories and symbols of the Christian faith. The power, the beauty and the dynamic motion of dance have opened up for me the experience of God. It is my desire that these ''reflections of a dancing priest'' will prove helpful to dancers who would like to use their art as a means of religious expression, to liturgists whose movement/ritual imagination may be inspired and to the many faithful people who want to become a ''Dancing People of God.''

CHAPTER 1
Theological Perspectives

*C*reation—"In the beginning God created. . . ."
In a creation-centered theology, the initial presumption is that creation
is God's way of expressing godself; it is the way God is manifested as a
Being-in-relation. God's identity is established as one who communicates with human creation. The primary question, then, becomes
"How does God communicate and how does the human person respond?" What are the ways to dialogue, to respond to God's self-
communication? This, of course, presupposes a belief that God exists,
a God who reveals godself, who wishes to communicate love, word,
life. This is a rather large presumption, but one which is affirmed in a
context of faith. From such a perspective the question is asked, "How
does God communicate the God-reality? How does God share and
reveal life?" The first way, because of its temporal precedence, is in
creation. It is through the very creativity of God that the world came
to be. The tangible, material creation reveals the Creator. In its
multiplicity, the variety of species, the beauty, the simplicity, the first
Artist is revealed. The act of creation is expressive of the reality of
God; the world as sacrament of God's love reveals One who is related
to the human person through a reality that one can see, touch and
love. God is given in creation: water, sky, mountains, animals,
flowers, colors, shapes and form. God communicates through *this*
world, *this* time, and *this* space. God communicates in a way we can
understand; the world of creation is the language of the human
dialogue with God.

Creation, however, is not something static. It is dynamic. What
discloses creation as dynamic is life. Life has to do with growth and
change. In the cycles of birth, life, death and rebirth is found the context of the whole created world. It is movement that reveals life and
creation. The Spirit hovering over the waters is the generative moment

in the Creation story. The planets, stars, day and night, rivers and oceans, the interior of all living things move and say, "Here is Life!" Even in the stillness of the human heart there is the movement of the living Spirit. In creation, then, God chooses to be revealed through movement—through growth and change, through living and dying and coming back to life. All of life is movement. Without it there is no life. Through creation, then, the human person is capable of understanding God's self-communication. Through movement, one captures the sense of the "spirit of God." The spirit that is described as wind, breath and fire reveals God as moving, creative, restoring and life-giving. The spirit of God is the spirit of creativity, that which gives new life, shape, and form to what was not there before. Creation, then, is the first mode of God's self-communication.

It should be clear that someone who is involved in creation, one who gives shape and form to the material of this earth, one who is called "artist" may feel very close to God in the action of artistic creation. Artists may see themselves as "imitators of God's creativity." They use the materials of this world to create. Clay, word, color, stone, flesh are the givens of the artist's world. The dancer uses the human body to create changing shapes and forms. The dancer/ choreographer is one who yields to the limits of time and space in order to fashion either the fine clarity of a human emotion, or some abstract patterns, intriguing in themselves but devoid of any recognizable personal expression. Dance can be many different things but its instrument is always the flesh and blood, the "embodied" reality of living, human beings. The dancer and the dance are one and the same. Because the materials of creation are part of the vocabulary of human life, we struggle to understand the artist's communication. There is a universality about all the arts that one can recognize in any experience of sound, color, form, movement, shape. There is a common human experience that is awakened by an artist's creation of something that simply was not there before. Artists narrow a particular reality with their vision, thereby expanding the vision of the one who receives the creation as well as expanding the subject/object reality and offering it focus and new life.

It is difficult to articulate verbally the vision and reality of any artistic expression without experiencing it. The dance, however, offers an even greater challenge because of the nature of the medium itself. The dancer is captured in a fleeting moment, moving through time and space. The moment can never be repeated or recorded in the same way, with the same immediacy. Any art is an act of self-relevation and self-gift, as the initial act of creation was. Dancers give themselves away for the sake of a "greater reality," becoming one with a rhythm, a pattern, a vision, an emotional expression. With the dance are blended so many of the other arts—music, painting, sculpture, drama, etc. The total experience calls forth an articulation that can not be captured in descriptive language. The work of art must be seen, felt, heard, touched, and yet we will attempt to express as best we can the elusive act of creation, using words that can not do justice to the simplicity and honesty of the human gesture.

The artist shares in the creativity of God and for that reason can open up to others the mystery of God's revelation in specific human terms. Through art, the artist enables another to "see" into the beauty, the pain of life that must be deeply rooted in God's creation. The artist offers many different visions of the reality of God's presence in the world. A multi-faceted diamond reveals a brilliance of the whole and yet each face of the diamond gives us an entry into the brilliance of the whole. Each work of art can offer an avenue of approach into the splendor, the majesty, the simple, yet complex beauty of the Creator, the Divine Artist.

INCARNATION

The second way in which God communicates Godself to the world is through Incarnation. From a Christian perspective, God becomes one of us, invests fully in this creation. God speaks a human language. It took four centuries for the Church to define the two natures of Jesus Christ . . . "fully human . . . fully divine." After sixteen more centuries people still struggle to understand the meaning of that primary Christian affirmation. It is clearly the most difficult, yet crucial reality that theologians have struggled with in attempting to translate the meaning of this divine/human reality into a language that people of faith can understand or at least begin to grasp. What does the Incarnation mean in people's day-to-day existence? The Fathers of the Church attempted to express what is at stake; if Jesus is not fully human, then there are parts of human existence that are not redeemed, that remain untouched by God's self-investment in Jesus. If Jesus is not fully divine, if he is less than this, then God has not invested fully in the redemptive action of Jesus. God has held back the unconditional love that expresses the core of God's being. The Incarnation, then, is an invitation to enter into the human condition as completely as possible so that one may share in the divine life. The paradox simply stated is, "The more human we become, the more divine we are." As difficult as this is to believe, it is still the great Christian mystery. There may be a strong resistance to this essential belief. People may so distrust themselves that belief is impossible, for it is much easier to make God and the human two totally distinct and separate realities, than to see the unity or inter-relatedness of the two in Jesus and, therefore, in the human person.

My own conviction of the truth of the incarnational mystery comes from Ignatian spirituality. In the *Spiritual Exercises* of St. Ignatius of Loyola, there is a strong emphasis on "finding God in all things." This is not "pantheism" that Ignatius preaches. It is rather an invitation to discover God as the ground and source of all creation and the very root of the human. It is an entrance into the vision of a world charged with the life of God as the Jesuit poet Gerard Manley Hopkins expresses in his poem, "God's Grandeur":

> The world is charged with the grandeur of God.
> It will flame out, like shining from shook foil.[1]

The Christian artist has a keen sense of this incarnated reality. As he or she creates with word or song, with clay or paints, with stone or flesh, there can be an overpowering sense of God in the human. Creation and Incarnation become one. One discovers the reality of God's self-revelation becoming flesh in the act of creation. The Incarnation that happened once and for all in Jesus is somehow carried on or disclosed as the artist reveals the divine spark in the human act of creation. A personal illustration of this may be helpful:

In my early days as a dancer, I had the opportunity to work with a very talented artist. There was a quality about her movement that I can only describe as "spiritual;" it was ethereal and visibly transcendent. There was etched on her face and in her eyes the vision of a reality beyond the present moment but rooted in it. And yet it was strangely clear that the beauty of this moment was conceived in deep expression of human agony. This perception of the transcendent so firmly rooted in the enfleshed experience of struggle in this one life, enabled me to say: "This moment is clearly from God." It was a perception of the beauty of the human and the divine not in competition, not looking for escape from each other but simply merging as one. For me it was an experience of Incarnation. What I saw and realized in that dance studio that day was this: human gestures, human emotions, human hopes and dreams, the human heart and human agony are now God's own modes of expression. Indeed, the human reveals the divine as the divine discloses the human.

If God had taken the human person so seriously as to invest the Creator, to incarnate godself in the person of Jesus of Nazareth, there are a number of implications that follow, especially for those who use the dance as their mode of artistic expression and communication:

1. The instrumentality of divine/human communication is the flesh and blood of human lives, persons who are not disembodied but rather "embodied" selves.

2. The response to God's initiative of incarnate love in the context of worship will demand a response of the whole person, not just an intellectual assent.

3. The human word/gesture/symbol becomes the divine milieu. Our embodied communication to each other "in God's name," with God's story, discloses the divine communication of graciousness.

My own journey as an artist in the Church has been a continual attempt to believe and affirm in myself the truth of the Incarnation; that in yearning to express the deepest core of human life through the gestures, the movement, the dances I make, I am in touch with and bring to expression the mystery of God's creative and incarnate life. And so I continue the journey.

CHAPTER 2

Liturgical Danced Prayer

O ver the past twenty years, the growing movement in liturgical dance has evoked varied responses from different quarters of the Church. From joyful acceptance to distasteful rejection, liturgical dance has elicited impassioned responses of "We want more!" or "It doesn't belong!" Like the initial and sometimes continued reaction to guitars in church, the reaction to liturgical dance is complicated by people's expectations of how the church's worship, especially Eucharistic worship, "should be." A narrow concept of worship will not allow for much space or alteration of the "normal" way of doing things. The very nature of ritual, in its familiar and repetitive content and chronology, mitigates against bringing in something new. Given the basic distrust and discomfort with bodily, physical expression, it is only reasonable that more use of the body than is explicitly required is not something to be accepted or encouraged. The contradiction within this stance, that human ritual must be "embodied" but at the same time "disembodied" (entirely spiritual), is apparent in two recent documents of the Roman Catholic Church. In the document on *Art and Environment in Catholic Worship,* the Bishops Committee on the Liturgy speaks of the need for gesture, movement (dance) in the liturgy precisely because the liturgy is a human ritual.

> . . . because good liturgy is a ritual action, it is important that worship space allow for movement. Processions and interpretations through bodily movement (dance) can become meaningful parts of the liturgical

celebration if done by truly competent persons in the manner that benefits the total liturgical action. (59).

An opposing view is given in *Notitiae* (Notices, 1975), a publication of the Sacred Congregation for Sacraments and Divine Worship. *Notitiae* are essays commenting on specific areas of Canon Law. The author of this unsigned essay, written in Italian, sees dance in Western culture in only two ways: associated with "courtship rituals" or performance as in "artistic ballet."[2] Neither of these dance expressions is seen as appropriate in a liturgical context. In Eastern cultures, where dance is part of the ordinary life expression, it is begrudgingly accepted in the liturgy.

There are a number of problems with the analysis of dance in the *Notitiae* commentary and they need to be dealt with in detail. In this context, however, initial comment is given:

1. The Church has always used dance in its ritual. In processions, bows, blessings, prostrations, changes of posture, the liturgy of the Church has "embodied" its prayer. When gesture and movement are used in a functional way, they are just that. When they are used in a formal, ritualistic way they become "dance." Walking, for example, is movement, in and of itself. Walking in procession is a dance because of its formal and symbolic structure.

2. The attitude toward the body in the *Notitiae* is strikingly negative. The body is seen as the cause of sin. This attitude ignores an "Incarnational theology" that says that the whole person is redeemed by the saving action of Jesus Christ. The major liturgical document of the Second Vatican Council, the *Constitution on the Sacred Liturgy* states,

   > Mother Church earnestly desires that all the faithful should be led to that full, conscious and active participation in liturgical celebrations which is demanded by the very nature of liturgy. (14.)

   Full participation is only possible in ritual if people are encouraged to be "embodied" selves rather than "disembodied" spirits.

3. It is imperative that people experience a prayerful use of the body in such a way that gives praise and glory to the One who is the Creator of the human, the whole person, and who chose to take on human flesh and blood in Jesus Christ.

The pastoral challenge that arises in response to the negative attitude toward the body, so evident in the *Notitiae*, is one of thoughtful and sensitive education. People need to know that their physical presence is the primary way of being in the world, being in relation to others and to God. There is a great need of affirmation of the whole person especially in the liturgical context, for it is in liturgy that we engage in a dialogue of the whole self with God. An educated and informed understanding of the dynamics of ritual can lead to a deeper appreciation of what people are doing as they gather together to worship.

WHAT IS LITURGICAL DANCE?

One of the problems that has arisen regarding liturgical dance is the many different interpretations of what it is. From highly choreographed, "full-length" ballets, performed by experienced dancers and inserted into the liturgy at some point (in place of the homily, at the preparation time, or after communion), to simple offerings of prayer done by untrained but well-intentioned individuals, "liturgical dance" has been a catch-all term for every kind of movement, gesture or dance that happens during a liturgy (most frequently, Eucharistic liturgy). Two of the most influential people in Roman Catholic liturgical dance, Carla deSola and Gloria Weyman have written about some of the norms, the prerequisites and intentions of liturgical dance. These works have been extremely helpful in guiding those interested in liturgical dance. A recent work by Lawrence Johnson, *The Ministers of Music,* has a brief but excellent analysis of the role of the dancer in Christian worship.

My part of this book is an attempt at some synthesis of the various approaches to liturgical dance and an opportunity to provide a framework for continued discussion. It is especially important that liturgical dance be considered as a serious contribution to the liturgical life of the Church and not be rejected as not essential. The following analysis will open up the definition of liturgical dance and provide some clarity in the understanding of its function and purpose.

My personal preference is to speak of Liturgical Danced Prayer. There is a reason for this. Each word has a descriptive purpose in defining this activity in liturgy.

Liturgical

Liturgy, from its root meaning, is "something that people do together." It is a common action with an expressed purpose. In a religious context, the word signifies people who come together (the assembly) to give expression to their faith in specific actions, using signs and symbols that are "meaning-ful." In the Eucharistic Liturgy, for example, people of faith come together to sing, pray, listen, respond, and share a meal because these words and actions express their belief in a God who communicates through the Jesus-reality. Although Eucharistic liturgy—giving thanks to God for, with and through Jesus, is the principal way or worship in the Church—it is not the only form of liturgy. There are other ways in which people assemble to express their faith in ritual actions with meaningful symbols, such as Liturgy of the Hours, the other sacraments and special rituals. What is primary is that liturgy be expressive of the faith of a community.

> **In the restoration and promotion of the sacred liturgy, this full and active participation by all the people is the aim to be considered before all else . . . (Constitution on the Sacred Liturgy, 14).**

The prayer of the assembly as the Body of Christ needs to be attended to if the liturgy is going to do what is its purpose and intent. This emphasis on the prayer of the whole assembly does not mean that everyone must be doing everything, that everyone sings every piece of music, that all pray the Eucharistic prayer together, that all movement be done by the entire assembly. This extreme posture denies the human need and ritual dynamic of "roles" within the assembly. There are certain members of the assembly who are designated to act "on behalf of" the community, such as presider, lectors, other ministers, musicians and dancers. When the dance has been used in the liturgy, it has struggled for acceptance for the following reasons: a) Not

everyone can do it, b) The people who do it are either performers without faith or faith-filled people without training, c) the visual orientation of dance as opposed to the aural orientation of music demands an attention that can "distract" from the liturgical action. To these criticisms the following responses are offered: a) There is a language of non-verbal, symbolic prayer that is accessible to the whole assembly. This language must be cultivated and explored in relation to the gestures of the presider and the other ministers. There are, indeed, "gestures, actions and bodily attitudes" (Constitution on the Sacred Liturgy, 30) appropriate to the whole assembly; b) The role of the dancer must be explored in specific terms of the integration of dance into the entire liturgical action. These dances need to be balanced by the movement participation of presider and assembly. This would mitigate against "having a liturgical dance" as if it were separate from the ritual flow. It would also guard against a superimposition of gestures or dance in places in the ritual that have their intrinsic action already defined, such as dancing the *Lamb of God* when the principal action is the breaking of bread and pouring out of the wine; c) A crucial challenge to liturgical education is the acknowledgement of the different media to communicate to people through their distinct modalities. If, for example, musical liturgy is normative for all liturgy, then music is a primary modality of the liturgy. One way in which people pray in the liturgy is meant to be through music. It is not an arbitrary decision whether to have music. It does not simply add to the celebration. It is, rather, the privileged way of celebrating.

Within this modality there is a great variety of expressions. Gregorian chant and music for guitar evoke certain emotional reactions because of musical structure and the way in which the different expressions have been used in the liturgy. Acclamations, hymns, responses, sung Eucharistic prayers, all will have a certain power to communicate through the musical modality but in fidelity to the form in which they are composed. A problem that arises in the proclamation of the Word in the liturgy is the failure to recognize the variety of literary forms in the one modality of the spoken word. Certain passages of scripture are poetry, some drama, and some stories. These forms are not meant to be fused into one sound but should be faithful to the form of composition. In the visual arts in liturgy, the same principle applies. The visual arts need to communicate according to their distinct modalities; dance happens in space and time. One way in which dance communicates in the liturgy is by "enlivening" the space where the ritual takes place and "intensifying" the time in which it unfolds. It is a way of saying, "This time is sacred, this space in sacred." The necessary education for the assembly is in allowing communication to take place through many different modalities; sound, sight, touch, taste, smell.

In summary, then, the overarching liturgical principle that will assist the appropriate use of liturgical dance is *whatever is done and by whom must enhance or support those actions and symbols that are intrinsic to the community's celebration.* The point of this principle demands a critical look at the flow and development of the liturgy. It is saying that liturgical movement should be intrinsic to the liturgy, not just super-imposed "pretty" movements that could be easily discarded. Just as three chord pieces of music, played by well-intentioned beginners, do not provide a suitable context and expression of prayer, so too the use of dance, movement and gesture in a too facile way will only hinder the prayer of the assembly and not enrich it. A quotation from *Art and Environment in Catholic Worship* says this well:

> If an art form is used in liturgy it must aid and serve the action of liturgy since liturgy has its own structure, rhythm and pace: a gathering, a building up, a climax, and a descent to dismissal. It alternates between persons and groups of persons between sound and silence, speech and song, movement and stillness, proclamation and reflection, word and action. The art form must never seem to interrupt, replace, or bring the course of liturgy to a halt . . . If, however, an art form is used to enhance, support and illumine a part or parts of the liturgical action or the whole action, it can be both appropriate and rewarding (25).

Danced

A simple definition of dance is "rhythmic movement." The most narrow definition of dance includes only those movements which are done to a recognizable rhythm and meter, in a formal structure, with a specific intention. This narrow definition looks at someone jumping around erratically and denies that the movement is dance because there is no immediately recognizable order. The same definition looks at the repetitive but structured "jumping around" of an Indian ritual and recognizes "dance" because of rhythm, order and intention. A broader definition of dance, however, allows any movement or gesture done by a human body to be a dance no matter if it is the least recognizable rhythm and devoid of any specific form. What makes it "dance" is that the person intends it to be seen as such. (Someone sitting on stage for fifteen minutes in stillness and then raising a finger, arm or leg is considered a dance of enormous power by many. In fact, for many post-modern choreographers, if it looks like what we *expect* dance to be, it can't be any good).

This spectrum of understanding is only the first source of confusion in translating this category of human experience into the liturgy. The second source of fear, anxiety, and disapproval comes from the association that dance has with fleshly eroticism and courtship rituals.

There are many who can accept the principle of liturgical movement but are extremely resistant to calling it "dance." As long as we do not name the beast, we are on safe ground.

The third source of anxiety comes from the association that dance has with the irrational. When one speaks of "dancing at Mass" people immediately conjure up images of uncontrolled frenzy as in some pagan ritual. The liturgy of Christians is by its nature an "ordered" ritual which demands a certain quality and energy in its words and actions. When there is a deviation from this "restraint" some people experience a loss of reverence. The struggle between involving the head or the heart in worship has been a reality for many centuries.[3] The challenge is to find a balance; to find a quality and energy in worship that is faithful to "celebration" and to "prayer."

One of the most positive contributions dance has to make to liturgy is an awareness of the "rhythm" of ritual. There is tremendous power in the rhythms of worship, not only in the music that the community hears or sings but also in the balance among word, silence and action. The most singular compliment one hears these days in regard to a "successful" liturgy is that it had a flow and rhythm about it. Somehow people can be caught up in that flow and experience the celebrative event. A good example of the power of rhythm is seen in

many entrance processionals. Although processionals have always been meant to be stately dances, most would rather have them be functional "walks" without any regard to the underlying rhythms of the accompanying music. In a procession at a recent liturgy, the deacon carried the book with a simple rhythm in his step, left-right-left-together, right-left-right-together. There was extraordinary power in his presentation of the Gospel book because he had entered into the rhythm of the ritual. He let the music and the movement be the expression of joy and celebration.

In speaking of liturgical danced prayer, we refer to all those movements, gestures and rhythmic expressions of the body that are not merely functional but rather have an intention of prayer and communal celebration. They are the moments in liturgy which use the symbolic language of the non-verbal to cry out on behalf of the whole community, to express a depth of human experience that can not be spoken in words. Moments of sorrow, anguish, of faith-filled joy and ecstasy that are given life and liveliness through the body are the "stuff" of liturgical danced prayer. From the simple lifting up of the arms at the beginning of the Eucharistic prayer to a more festive dance at the closing of the celebration, liturgical danced prayer can capture and express the hearts of the faithful if it is allowed to speak and be seen for what it is, a valid form of prayer.

Prayer

One of the simplest definitions of prayer is given by Jean LaPlace, S.J. in a brief booklet, *Prayer*. He says that it is "a dialogue of the heart with God."[4] It is a dialogue that involves attentive listening and response. It is the heart that listens and responds. The heart, here, is a symbol for the whole person—mind and body. The call of prayer is a give and take between an embodied person and a living incarnate God. The language of prayer is both verbal and non-verbal. As Paul says in the letter to the Romans, "The spirit helps us in our weakness because we do not know how to pray; but the spirit groans for us with groanings that can not be expressed in speech" (Rom. 8).

Even if private prayer is sometimes an escape from the corporeal, embodied reality into a world of mental or affective ecstasy in contemplation, communal, liturgical prayer must be embodied. In liturgy, voices need to speak and bodies need to move to bring faith to expression. The liturgy is not meant to be an aerobics class, but it can be a more active and living experience of the presence of a living God, if the body is allowed to speak its language of faith and not be excluded because of preconceived notions of what prayer "should" be.

It is clear that the roots of Judeo-Christian prayer reveal a prayer of the whole person. The psalms speak of the body as part of the prayer dialogue. "You have changed my mourning into dancing" (Ps. 30). "Praise the Lord with timbrel and dance" (Ps. 150). The prayer of the Hebrews is a physical prayer that reveals the need to speak to God, to listen to God and to respond to God with a total, unprotected innocence, with the honesty of the whole person moving, reaching, touching. This God chose to be incarnated in Creation and, in Jesus, speaks the incarnational language of the body. God knows and hears the cry of the whole person—not merely the spoken word, but also movement, reaching or touching. It is in the expression of prayer that comes from the whole person that one discovers the presence of a *living, moving, creative* God.

In summary, Liturgical Danced Prayer is those gestures and rhythmic movements that give expression to the faith of the community through a non-verbal communication among the members of the assembly as they gather to celebrate that faith in word and action. There are a number of implications that follow from this definition:

1. There are gestures and rhythmic movements that are appropriate for the whole assembly, some that are for the presider as leader of prayer and some that can be done by dancers who are part of or somehow represent the community.

2. Whatever gestures and rhythmic movements are chosen, the emphasis should be put on the non-verbal symbolic language of the liturgy rather than a "representational" use of movement. The dance should allow the symbols to speak.

3. Because there is already a ritual-movement structure in much liturgy, the use of more defined gestures or dance should be carefully integrated into the existing flow of the ritual action.

WHY LITURGICAL DANCED PRAYER?

Through "signs perceptible to the sense," the assembly is invited to "full, conscious and active participation" in the mystery of Christ's life, death and resurrection (Constitution on the Sacred Liturgy, 7, 14). In former times, the liturgy was a *drama* that unfolded before the eyes of interested but uninvolved spectators. The present trend is to identify the whole assembly as "actors" in the drama, or rather as "dancers" in this ritual dance of life, death and new life. It is one thing to speak *about* the themes of life, death, resurrection, salvation, and healing. It is another to enable people to experience the events, to engage them in the ritual action, so that the sacred events can be owned and claimed as personal and communal expressions of faith. It is the non-verbal, symbolic expression that can lead to this engagement, can open up a well of conscious and subconscious associations, can lead to a deepening awareness of the individual and communal role in the "mystery of faith."

This "engagement" of the faithful through non-verbal symbols, gestures and movement, leading to full participation is the primary reason for liturgical, embodied prayer. It is not to make the service "less boring," nor is it meant to be a novelty to attract people's attention. It is a way of entering into the liturgy as "event," as a vital celebration of human and divine hopes and dreams for the present and future. Through the affective, psychological processes of unconscious association, the symbol works as a common bond that unifies the individuals as one and, at the same time, allows the individual his or her own personal associations in his or her own experience. The powerful symbol of ashes, for example, unites the community in reflection/experience of penance, vulnerability, or mortality but each individual has his or her own associations and specific expressions of those experiences. An adult who receives ashes is taken back to childhood experiences of ashes, death, passing through years in the conscious or unconscious reflection of a moment because of the continuity of one symbol.

The assembly needs to be engaged through liturgical movement that is consistent with its role. Whatever can be done to facilitate this participation will enrich the liturgy. The bridge between the assembly and the symbol comes from those "symbol-bearers" in the liturgy who through their actions bring the symbols to life; presider, musicians, lectors, dancers. It is especially important that dancers, who have a more finely tuned instrument of non-verbal communication, awaken in the assembly the "kinesthetic" sense that enables them to move "with" the dancer without having to move themselves. It is these three elements of non-verbal expression that must be attended to if the liturgy is going to engage the whole person in prayer: the symbol, the assembly, and those designated in the assembly to express a fuller and more complex realization of the affective dimensions of liturgical celebration, such as sorrow, joy, longing and other human emotions.

HOW LITURGICAL DANCED PRAYER?

One of the most important developments in liturgical renewal in the past twenty years has been the rediscovery of the central role of sym-

bol in ritual. Bread that looks like bread, water that washes and refreshens, oil that heals the whole body, invite the assembly into the sacramental experience. These signs, "perceptible to the senses" need to be such. For effective ritual symbols must be allowed to speak. Paul Ricoeur speaks of symbols as "revealing" and "concealing." There is clarity and mystery at the same time. A symbol, if it is effective, is what it is but draws one into a level of meaning beyond the immediately perceived reality. A symbol must first "be what it is." It must be seen, tasted, touched, smelled—experienced as what it is. If a symbol is allowed to "be what it is," it has the potential for conscious and subconscious association. For example, when people gather to break bread and share a cup of wine there can be the visceral memory of what Eucharist is. There can be a real interplay between "ordinary" events and those that are ritualized through the use of symbols.

The reason that the symbolic structure of ritual is so important to the "how" of liturgical dance is that the primary symbol in any and every liturgy is the *body*. The individual persons gather together as embodied presences and symbolize the Body of Christ. For this primary symbol to work, the body must be allowed to be an integral part of the ritual action. It must in fact be the "locus of prayer." *Environment and Art in Catholic Worship* says:

> Among the symbols with which liturgy deals, none is more important than this assembly of believers (28). The most powerful experience of the sacred is found in the celebration and the persons celebrating, that is, it is found in the action of the assembly: the living words, the living gestures, the living sacrifice, the living meal (29).

As important as it is to use symbols that are perceptible to the senses, there remains the challenge to let the primary symbol come to life so that it can signify what it is meant to be, the Body of Christ.

In order to bring the assembly to its rightful place as the primary symbol through full and active participation, it is necessary to explore the actions, gestures, and bodily attitudes that are conducive to prayerful celebration and feasible for a heterogeneous group of persons. Psychology has taught us much about the non-verbal communication that precedes the verbal. Sitting in a closed, defensive position, arms and legs crossed, eyes or head darting around reveals unease, discomfort, or distraction. The non-verbal signals of coughs or rustling in seats tell a speaker that boredom is taking over. It is clear that a whole level of communication stems from the body and is pre-verbal. It is on this basic level of pre-verbal communication that the assembly must first be engaged. The following is a breakdown of the basic actions, gestures and attitudes accessible to the whole assembly:

1. Postures

Standing:	Primary attitude of respect, such as standing when one enters or leaves.
Sitting:	Attentiveness, ease, comfort for listening, reflecting.
Kneeling:	Humility, penance, servitude, clearly delineating difference of station.

2. Simple Gestures

Bowing:	Sign of reverence, respect
Prostration:	Dramatic sign of surrender, penance, unworthiness.
Genuflecting:	Same as kneeling
Joining hands:	Communal unity
Embracing:	Love, peace, healing
Blessing:	Sign of cross, or open palms, arms extended . . . grace and graciousness
Processing:	Journeying toward
Laying of hands:	Empowerment, healing
Turning of the body:	Change of focus to another significant action.
Praying:	Specific gestures with arms extended or hands clasped together.
Striking the breast:	Contrition, mercy

3. Rhythmic Movements

Processing:	Coordinating the movements with the music, using more complex step combination, such as the tripudium step (three steps forward one or two steps back).
Lifting of hands and arms:	In series of gestures for preface dialogue, our Father, psalm antiphon.
Simple circle dances:	Where space allows, basic grapevine and other folk forms that can be easily learned and adapted.

Within this basic schema of movement for the assembly there is room to explore gestures and movements that are appropriate for a specific assembly. The most important element is their integration into the entire liturgical flow.

All ministers in the liturgy are there to serve the prayer of the entire assembly. Their purpose is both functional and aesthetic. They are the primary "movers" of the liturgy because they direct, focus and enhance the action of a people gathering to hear the Word of God and share a meal in memory of Jesus. Because their roles are sometimes functional, sometimes aesthetic and sometimes both, there is a need for clarity and quality in the gestures and movements that are used. "Gestures which are broad and full in both a visual and tactile sense, support the entire symbolic ritual. When the gestures are done by the presiding minister, they can either engage the entire assembly and bring them into an even greater unity, or if done poorly, they can isolate" (Environment and Art in Catholic Worship, 56).

The capacity for non-verbal communication in the liturgy is greatly increased through the participation of trained dancers, not only those with professional training but those who have worked in the preparation of a specific liturgy and are recognized as movement people for that community. The dancer, given space and the larger vocabulary of movement, should be able to articulate through his or her body the subtle dynamics of penitence, hope, forgiveness, and joy, and to enliven the assembly through the shared kinesthetic sense. For those who want to use this form of expression, a question that arises is where is it most appropriate in the liturgy. The answer can be three-fold:

1. Places in the ritual that move . . . enlivening the space in a festive procession or recession, dancing the Alleluia to bring attention to the Gospel book . . . dancing with the incense in hands in evening prayer . . . presenting the gifts in a stylized procession.

2. Reflective moments that call for visualization . . . responsorial psalm or communion meditation. Great care must be exercised that it is done in such a way to lead the assembly into deeper reflection and not draw them from it.

3. Moments of intersection between the verbal and non-verbal . . . in the liturgy of the Word certain readings can be communicated more effectively with a visual drama/mime/dance presentation.

In the actual decision to use more extensive communication through dance in the liturgy, a great deal of pastoral and liturgical care should be exercised so that the dance fosters and enhances the prayer of the whole assembly.

It is at this point in the discussion of how to use liturgical danced prayer that one must address a crucial question. How important is the *form* of the ritual event? Does the form really matter? Or is the content the only important thing? Does the form of a meal really make a difference, for example, or is the content of the Mass enough to "carry" the ritual? Can form and content be divorced? This is a crucial question for the future of liturgical development, especially regarding the arts and how they are integrated in liturgical celebration. There are three ways of approaching this problem:

1. Emphasis on Form—It is only the form that makes a difference.

   The liturgy is neatly packaged; the symbols are clear but there is no spirit; active participation is lacking.

   In musical terms, there is an effective melody but the lyrics are empty. They do not express the faith of the community. Harmony and rhythm are sacrificed for the singable melody.

   In dance terms, there are pretty gestures or steps that are strung together into a series of movements but have no intrinsic connection or motivation.

2. Emphasis on Content—it is only the content that matters.

   The liturgy is effective no matter what it looks like. Even if it is not recognizable as a meal, the "grace of the sacrament" is still effective.

   In musical terms, there are wonderful lyrics but they are inconsistent with the musical form chosen.

   In dance terms, there is a great deal of emotion expressed but the movement itself does not support that intensity or kind of emotion.

3. Form reveals Content—Content clarifies Form—dialogue between the two.

   They can not be separated. The meal form creates the structure and reveals what the liturgy is. The verbal content clarifies the context and gives it a deeper, richer significance.

   In musical terms, the chosen rhythms, melodies, harmonies, lyrics work together to create one aesthetic experience.

   In dance terms, the movement reveals the meaning, and the meaning emerges from the chosen form.

There are practical implications that follow from the necessary integration of form and content. Here are some examples:

1. The physical space and the arrangement of the assembly in that space

will communicate the relative importance of the different elements in the liturgy. If people see only the backs of each others' heads, they can not consider others in the assembly as significant.

2. Despite the practical problems, there is a necessity for people to receive real bread and wine if they are to sense themselves being fed; sharing a meal. Receiving wafers in a "bread line" does not convey the richness of the symbol of Eucharist in its proper form.

3. Sections of the liturgy that have an essential musical form, such as responsorial psalm and Alleluia can not be recited and communicate accurately the affective content.

4. The movements of the ministers and assembly must be examined to see whether they communicate what they are supposed to communicate.

It is clear that more work needs to be done in this area of the inter-relationship of form and content in liturgical prayer. It is only when the two are indeed one that effective, dynamic and vital liturgy is possible. The following reflections will suggest some ideas for the selection of dance/movement forms in a liturgical context.

The vocabulary of dance is extraordinarily rich and varied and has come to be synthesized into different techniques with different bases of movement. All schools of movement, however, are rooted in "tension," the contraction and release of the muscles of the body. Dance means tension, drawing toward and moving away. All movement has its source in the "plie-tendu," the "bend and stretch" of the human body. Each technique, however, has come to be identified through its form. Along with the form comes a specific content or at least certain orientations. Thus, balletic movement is identified with beautiful, graceful, harmonious movement that is lyrical in quality, revealing a breadth, a lightness, an unearthly sense, a sense of soaring in space, barely touching the earth, balancing on pointe. The emphasis on line, pattern, and form that has been the vehicle for modern ballet choreographers uses the clarity of the body's form to visualize the music, thus giving another spatial orientation to the "content" which was previously only temporal. The style of Martha Graham, however, emphasizes the groundedness, the earthly sensuality of the body, locating the center of movement in the pelvis. The famous Graham "contraction" is a form of dance that reveals an intense expression of emotion, pain, sorrow, or joy. It is a way of the body's moving that betrays an interior life in touch with external reality. Each contemporary stylist, from the lyrical fall and recovery of Jose Limon, the abstraction of Merce Cunningham, to the idiosyncratic movement of many contemporary choreographers, chooses a form of movement to disclose what it is he or she means to communicate: an idea, an experience, a picture, a feeling. These particular movement styles are most often more finely tuned than the folk form that expresses the dimension of human life and emotion through a vocabulary of dance that is usually more accessible to the "folk" (although many folk dances are highly nuanced and take a great deal of expertise.)

In liturgical dance, in trying to decide which form or style will best reveal the content of prayer, there are a number of factors to be taken into consideration:

1. The dance is in ritual as servant. It is not there for itself or to stand on its own as a separate work of art (although this may be possible). There is already an existing "given" form that must be respected. It has a life and flow of its own. The dances for a festive liturgy in a large open space will be different from those in a formal Cathedral liturgy which has its own stylization and necessary rhythms.

2. The ordinary situation demands a working in conjunction with musicians and other liturgical planners. Most often there is a given musical form as well as an overall form. A four square hymn, a lilting folk melody, a dramatic psalm or a Brubeck "Alleluia" will elicit different choreographic responses by the nature of their rhythms, melodies, and texts.

3. Because of the necessary training and discipline involved in ballet and modern dance, the ordinary approach is to use folk forms for the assembly and the untrained dancer. One has to recognize the limits and demands of a specific dance form.

In summary, the decision on form and style in liturgical dance depends on all the factors already mentioned. Sometimes a balletic grand-jeté, sometimes a contraction in sorrow, sometimes a simple folk step is most appropriate. It is the whole context of prayer and celebration, in concert with the rhythm and flow of the ritual, that must always be taken into consideration.

CHAPTER 3

Dances of the Seasons

The liturgical celebrations during the seasons provide variety, color, texture, emotion, and richness of theme to what would be a rather unexciting "ordinary" time. Each season has its own particular symbols as well as those that are part of the ritual throughout the year, such as bread and wine, water, and oil. In Advent, the symbols are darkness and light; at Christmas, light and birth, evergreens and angelic choirs; in Lent, ashes and palms; in Easter, water, light, oil, flowers, and signs of new life; at Pentecost, fire, wind, and dancing people. There is a dramatic sequence to the events of the year that call forth special ritual response in symbolic moments. These "moments" are most often built into the rituals of the year, such as the Easter vigil. The problem that often arises, however, is that somehow these symbols are blurred and do not speak clearly. Many persons who have used liturgical danced prayer have discovered that gestures, movements, and dances in some form can indeed make the symbols of the seasons "come alive" and "speak" to the assembly. Because these celebrations are so special, they demand a special attention to the symbols and the way in which these symbols are allowed to communicate. Dancers in the liturgy serve as "symbol-bearers;" (the first and foremost symbol being the human body itself . . . a body that is called to be the place of divine and human interaction). A look at some of these seasonal celebrations can yield specific suggestions to make them expressive of the human desire to communicate with God and God's desire to speak an incarnational language.

ADVENT/CHRISTMAS — "The people who walked in darkness have
seen a great light" (Is. 8)

The primary symbols of the Advent season are darkness and light. It is
a season of expectation and hope that is expressed in the flickering
lights of candles glowing in the darkness to the enduring hope captured in the symbol of the "Advent wreath," a circle of evergreens,
claiming a promise soon to be fulfilled and a longing that will never
die.

A traditional song of the Advent season is *O Come, O Come
Emmanuel.* It has been the source of many Advent processionals.
What I would suggest is a simple walking pattern with a pause or lunge
on the Rejoice! Rejoice! section of the song. What can make the processional beautiful and interesting, however, is the movement of the
lights. This can be done holding the candles in both hands or one,
moving them in a clockwise or counter-clockwise direction. With the
Advent wreath carried in the middle of the processioners there can
seem to be the effect of the lights dancing around the wreath. Once
one verse is established in its movement, a simple choreographic
device that can be used is geometric patterns that change the visual
perception but do not confuse the dancers with extra "steps." The
basic pattern can be done around the altar in a circle or using diagonal
lines through the celebration space. Even the most inexperienced
choreographer can devise an interesting processional movement with
a simple walking base, some upper arm/body movements, and the use
of geometric patterns. This procession of lights for the Advent season
can be an effective and solemn way to engage the assembly in the symbols of light and darkness. An advantage is that this does not demand
trained dancers, but can be done by as many members of the community willing to learn and practice.

Many of the readings during the Advent season speak of God's
glory. Another effective use of the symbol of light would be to keep
the electric lights extinguished even after the opening processional. As
the liturgy of the Word continues, a few more candles are lit. The
Alleluia proclamation could then become a dance of lights around the
Gospel book. This would bring to expression the Word as Light in the
lives of the faithful people; "your Word is a lantern." There is a
beautiful *Alleluia* setting in Peloquin's *Lord of Life* that is solemn,
reverential, and very suitable to the theme of the Word Incarnate in
the Advent season. Again, there could be a simple movement of the
feet, a basic walking pattern, with more movement of lifting, lowering, turning, and passing the light as it shines on the Gospel book.
book.

All through the liturgy, during the preparation of gifts, the creed,
and so on, more lights could be lit. The gradual impression of light

building can be an effective means of having the assembly "come alive" to the light. By the conclusion of the liturgy the space would be ablaze with light. At this point, as a closing expression of faith, the song "City of God" from the St. Louis Jesuits' *Lord of Light* could be sung and danced. The lyrics speak of the light in the darkness, our tears turned into dancing, and other appropriate expressions of the Advent season. Depending upon the assembly, space, and time of preparation, this could be danced by those trained in the community or be simplified as a congregational dance given the requirements of space, time for preparation and openness to this kind of communal prayer expression. If it is impossible with the assembly, it is possible to use a simple but lively dance in a triple meter that many could do with willingness and preparation. This closing song and dance would express the primary symbol of a people who share their faith, their hope, their love, and their desire to "build the City of God."

Alternative Advent Suggestions

First Sunday-Year A: Begin the liturgy with the proclamation of the first reading Is. 2, 1-5. The image is walking together in the light of the Lord, streaming toward God's holy mountain. Immediately following the proclamation (ideally done in some other gathering place) the whole assembly or selected members and ministers would "go up with joy to the house of the Lord." Carrying the symbols of the season, the procession would in fact *do* what the first reading and psalm are speaking about; a joyful journey in faith and hope. A simple tripudium step; three forward one back could be the basis of this easy, rhythmic procession. Another new addition to the musical repertory is Peloquin's "Let us Go Rejoicing" from his *Songs of Israel II.*

   Third Sunday-Years A and C: There are certain readings that are meant to be simply "listened" to and reflected on. There are others, however, that can validly be "expressed" through mime, drama or dance. There is something about certain readings that calls for an appropriate visualization as well as a clear proclamation. In the third Sunday of Advent the theme of rejoicing is most explicit. In Isaiah 35, 1-6 and Zephaniah 3, 14-18, the readings use images of physical exultation, of life-giving expression. These readings could be "interpreted" by competent members of the community who have some training and background in mime or dance. The important caution, however, is that it not be a *literal* interpretation, using gestures or movements that say the same thing as the verbal text. The idea of this kind of interpretation is to capture the underlying emotions and conflicts and give them life through the movement. It is not to "picture" or "act out" what the words are saying. Its purpose is to enliven the spirit, not to burden it with repetitive images. The difficulty is that this kind of interpretation demands much planning and work with the reader of the text. Because there is no musical support, the rhythm of the language and the dancer's body have to mesh into an expressive unity. This is a most difficult liturgical dance and yet it seems to be a frequent addition to liturgies. Anyone who feels "moved by the spirit" comes forward to "interpret" the reading or the psalm. Such movement can be a distraction to the community. Because this interpretation demands so much coordination it demands sufficient preparation to enable the movement to speak its own language and not be imitative of the verbal language.

In Isaiah 35, for example, there are very clear and precise images: the desert blooming, feeble hands, weak knees, eyes of the blind opened, ears of the deaf cleared. The literal way of presenting this reading would be an attempt to find non-verbal images that correspond to the verbal images. One would be at pains to find explicit images for blindness, deafness, or weak knees. It is better to leave this to the imagination of the listener. An alternative is for two dancers to reveal the underlying expectation, excitement, and miraculous joy that stems from the experience of God's transformation. The challenge is to bring alive the emotional content of the reading and bring that to expression for those who are hearing and feeling that excitement. Meeting the challenge with this kind of liturgical movement is rewarding if it is done well. It enables the living Word to come to life.

First Sunday-Year B: The first reading of this liturgy, Isaiah 63, has been set to music by the St. Louis Jesuits (Redeemer Lord, *Lord of Light*). The driving rhythms, and the musical dissonance make this a very interesting piece of danceable liturgical music. (Often the unchanging rhythms of much liturgical music do not aid the dynamics of dance.) Through music and movement the Isaiah passage could be effectively communicated.

The climax of the Advent season is the celebration of the birth of Christ, the Incarnation. On this feast, it is especially appropriate to "incarnate" the Church's liturgy through movement prayer. Christmas is a season of wonder. The liturgy of this season needs to capture this sense of wonder, especially as it is embodied in the lives of children.

The *Directory for Masses with Children* encourages, "the development of gestures, postures, and actions . . . in view of the nature of the liturgy as an activity of the entire man and in view of the psychology of children" (33). It goes on to say that "the processional entrance of the children with the priest may help them to experience a sense of the communion that is thus constituted. The participation of at least some of the children in the procession with the book of the gospels makes clear the presence of Christ who announces his word to the people. The procession of children with the chalice and gifts expresses clearly the value and meaning of the presentation of gifts. The communion procession, if properly arranged, helps greatly to develop the piety of children" (34). The liturgy of Christmas should embrace these instructions and let the children give expression to their wonder in specific shape and form. There are numerous Christmas carols that can be used in procession. The story of Christmas can be told through different carols with the children dancing or miming. The origin of the "carol" is rooted in dance forms that were used in conjunction with the music. The Christmas liturgy would be an excellent opportunity to use the musical settings designed for children, such as Peloquin's "Unless you become . . ." This work affords many opportunities for movement acclamation, especially during the Alleluia and Eucharistic prayer.

The Advent/Christmas season is rich with symbols of hope, of longing, of wonder and promise. In the liturgies of this season, gesture, movement, and dance can incarnate what is hoped for and what has already been fulfilled in the coming of Christ.

LENT

The Lenten Season has its own richness of symbolic expression beginning with the celebration of ashes and culminating with the powerful
symbols of Holy Week. It is a season in the Church's liturgy that allows
the experience of the life, death and resurrection of Jesus to be
remembered in the lives of the assembled faithful. It is most important
during this season that the assembly be engaged in embodied prayer
so that they may experience their unique participation in the Easter
event. The renewed place of the Catechumenate during this season
has been helpful in letting the assembly claim the process of conversion as its own. The following are some suggestions for the involvement of the whole assembly as well as specific examples of dance during the Lenten/Easter season. It is a time of penitence, journeying,
growth in self-knowledge, a time to deepen one's knowledge of the
person of Jesus, especially in his humanity, a time to celebrate the
ultimate victory of life over death. It is a time to dance.

Ash Wednesday

This day that begins the Lenten season has the power of linking the past and looking forward to the future. The symbols are strong and clear. It is important that people see the burning of last year's palms so that there is a link with the past experience of Lenten conversion. (The cyclic nature of human ritual needs to be brought out more clearly.) Bread and wine should be seen and tasted as food for the journey. If possible, the signing with ashes should be done by members of the assembly to each other so that the symbol may be touched, felt, and seen. The liturgy can begin with a proclamation of Joel's "call to repentance" from within the assembly. The presider enters in silent procession and prostrates himself before the assembly. The members of the assembly kneel to express their need for conversion and repentance. There is time for silent prayer. On rising, the presider invites the community to further reflection and all sing a selection such as "Grant to us, O Lord" by Lucien Deiss. Following the homily and silent reflection, the presider burns some palm, blesses the ashes and invites the assembly to sign each other as a beginning symbol of solidarity with the Lord and with each other during this Lenten journey. At some point in the liturgy a single member of the assembly could dance, "Be Not Afraid" as an expression of hope and trust during the Lenten season. People can be drawn more deeply into the truth and beauty of the words of this song and the shared human experience they articulate.

The Sundays of Lent

The Liturgy of the Word during the Lenten season offers many opportunities for creative proclamation. The long gospels of John during Cycle A can be communicated through drama, mime or dance. A model of this kind of presentation is given in the work of the *Fountain Square Fools*. This group of professional actors, mimes and dancers has integrated the gospel story with imagination, energy, and conviction. The groups' portrayal of the parable of the *Prodigal* is exceptionally powerful.

The following are some suggestions for dance in the Sundays of Lent:

1st Sunday: The theme in all cycles is the temptation of Jesus in the desert. The song, *Jesus the Lord*, can be used as a response to the gospel reading. The slow, reflective antiphon repeated four times can lead the assembly into a simple gesture prayer. The music breathes the name Jesus and the gestures/movement should come as an extension of the rhythmic pulse set up by the breathing in and out on the name, Jesus. (It is important for those who design the movements for the assembly to explore all the possibilities of raising and lowering the hand and arms, so that all gestures do not look and feel alike.)

2nd Sunday: The theme in all cycles is the Transfiguration. Michael Joncas' setting, *On Eagle's Wings*, captures the spirit of this theme of transformation, light, and special protection. This particular piece of music with its intricate rhythms demands a certain expertise of the dancers who perform it. If the movement is to be faithful to the form and intent of the musical composition, it is important that the choreographer recognize the complexity of the music and not trivialize it with a too basic movement. The choreography for this piece in the repertoire of the Boston Liturgical Dance Ensemble, for example, includes arabesques on half-pointe, en penché, Soutenu turns, attitudes en promenade and renverses. These movements are visible to the assembly but need trained dancers to execute them.

3rd Sunday: In Cycle A, the gospel is the woman at the well and the liturgy has a strong Baptismal theme. John Foley's *Come to the Water* can be an effective response to the liturgy of the Word and a bridge to the liturgy of the Eucharist. In a liturgy at St. James Cathedral in Brooklyn, New York, the Boston Liturgical Dance Ensemble danced with members of the assembly who had been trained the day before in a workshop. A white cloth twenty yards long was drawn through the building by twenty dancers. Working the cloth in an undulating motion, the dancers gave the impression of water flowing, enveloping the assembly with the symbol. Two dancers near the altar danced more complex movements. The cloth was drawn over them and then placed on the altar to become the altar cloth. The two dancers then presented the gifts to the presider and the liturgy continued.

The variety of themes during this season afford many more opportunities for non-verbal expressions. The theme of forgiveness and reconciliation can be embodied through gestures of healing, through enacting the gospel stories of reunion, through expressing the affective dimension of reconciliation in the psalms of the season (Pss. 23, 130, 137, 51, 34). The musical settings of these psalms very in style and will effect the movement interpretation. Certain musical forms are more conducive to the necessary tension within dance composition. Many of the psalm settings of Peloquin, for example, have a musical tension that elicits an expressive movement response.

Holy Week

Holy Week is clearly the highpoint of the Church's liturgical year. The celebration of the life, death and resurrection of Jesus demands a liturgy rich in word and action, mood and symbol. The Holy Week liturgies need to involve the whole person in prayer. The relaity of Passover is incarnated in bodies that move. This movement emerges naturally from the existing ritual and does not have to be super-imposed upon it. The following are examples of places in the ritual that call for "embodiment."

Passion Sunday

Procession with Palms: a) the whole community gathers outside the building and enters in procession carrying the palms. b) With the community already assembled, dancers carrying royal palms enter in rhythmic procession to "All Glory Laud and Honor." The procession uses a simple walking base, punctuated by lunges. The dancers open and close the palms, turn and reach with them. The royal palms have a majesty that conveys the solemnity of the occasion.

Proclamation of the Passion: There have been many different approaches to dramatic presentations of the Passion. One effective presentation that has been used employs a combination of dramatic reading and mime. A long purple cloth is used as the unifying symbol throughout. It functions as the cloth for the last supper and delineates the different places, the garden, the house of Annas, Pilate's palace. It becomes the cloth thrown over Jesus, the cross itself and then the burial cloth. The narrative is read by trained lectors and the dance/mime is done by dancers and actors. This particular rendering of the Passion has engaged the assembly with powerful emotion, even though they did not "do" anything.

The Assembly's Acclamations: The original Palm Sunday event had people in the streets of Jerusalem acclaiming Jesus as King. During the acclamations of the Eucharistic Prayer, the assembly should be invited to raise their arms with palms in hand, waving them with the words, "Hosanna in the Highest, blessed is he who comes in the name of the Lord," and at other points of acclamation.

Holy Thursday

Washing of Feet: An important gesture embodying the gospel which preceeds it. This is a case where form and content are inextricably bound. The command of Jesus to "love one another" is tied to a specific symbol of service. This sign should not be neglected for the sake of convenience or speed. It is also important that it be done in such a way that it is a visible sign to the whole assembly.

Preparation of Gifts: The symbols of bread and wine should be given an even greater emphasis on this night. A more elaborate procession may be called for. The symbols must be clearly visible and genuine; bread that is baked by someone in the community, wine held in a lovely carafe.

Transfer of the Eucharist: A simple but powerful movement that can engage people in reverence and prayer.

Stripping the Altar: This silent ritual has an extraordinary psychological effect on people. It can be a striking prelude to the experience of Good Friday.

Good Friday

Prostration: Prostration is an important gesture of penance, humility and dependence. The silent procession and the prostration is a stark beginning to the Good Friday liturgy.

Orations: "Let us kneel. Let us stand." The Good Friday liturgy tries to involve the assembly in postures that embody the reverence and respect for the solemnity of the celebration. The community should take time to kneel in silent prayer so that the movement "kneel-stand" is expressive of an attitude of reverence and respect rather than an empty gesture of inconvenient effort.

Veneration of the Cross: A movement that involves the whole assembly in procession and praise. It affords the opportunity to express an attitude of loving reverence not only for Jesus' sacrifice but for all of life which is embraced by the symbol of the cross.

EASTER VIGIL

On this night the Church uses all of its basic symbols to allow a rich experience of new life and hope. The elements of fire, water, bread, and wine become the sacramental manifestation of the presence of God. The form and structure of the celebration, from the lighting of the new fire, the procession of light, the proclamation of the exsultet, the stories of God's activity in the world, the baptismal event, to the new Passover meal that is shared, proclaim the single most important affirmation of the Christian faith. "He is risen. *Alleluia!*" All of the symbolic elements of this ritual are involved in this proclamation. That is why it is so important on this night to allow the symbols to speak. The following are some suggestions for an effective ritual:

Lighting of the Fire: If feasible, begin outside so that all can see the fire. The procession should only begin when all have their candles lit. The final acclamation should be intoned only when all have assembled in the celebration space. During the exsultet, candles should be kept burning.

The lights (electric) should be left off until the *Gloria*.

Liturgy of the Word: In darkness, except for the light of the paschal candle and any light necessary for the lector, the readings are proclaimed. For the Genesis reading, six lectors are stationed throughout the church, each with an unlit candle. As the story of creation begins, a dancer comes to the paschal candle and draws the light from the candle. He or she then goes to the next reader bringing the light. As each reader takes a day of creation, each receives a light. At the end of the seven days there are seven lights symbolizing the creation. The positions of these readers around the perimeter of the space can create the impression of being surrounded by creation.

Gloria: Out of the darkness comes a dancing people! As the final response to the Ezekiel reading is being sung, all the candles are lit again. As the Gloria is intoned, the first image the assembly has is women and men dressed in white and gold, dancing to this song of praise.

Alleluia: The first Alleluia of the Easter Season should be embodied in a joyful dance around the gospel book. This could be done as a procession with the book or as a special incensation with dancers moving around the book, carrying bowls of incense.

The entire liturgy of Easter cries out for the full participation of the assembly. In the baptismal and communion rites that follow the proclamation of the Word, the people should be engaged by the symbols in the acclamation, "Christ has died, Christ is risen, Christ will come again! Alleluia!" It is the task of those working with movement and gesture in liturgy to continue to find suitable ways to make the Easter event come to life.

PENTECOST

Pentecost gives another opportunity to ritualize the Easter event but where the focus of Easter is the proclamation, "Jesus is risen," the focus of Pentecost is "Where are God's people." This is the celebration of a people filled with the spirit of God. It is an appropriate time for dance as an expression of the joy, the ecstasy, and the liveliness of the Spirit. There are a number of musical settings appropriate for a festive opening procession. Peloquin's, *Lord, Send Out Your Spirit,* The Monks of the Weston Priory's, *Spirit Alive,* Peloquin's *Praise to the Lord,* have all been used by the Boston Liturgical Dance Ensemble as opening processionals to enliven the celebration space on this special feast. In these pieces, red material is used to suggest the tongues of fire and capture the breath, vitality and dynamic movement of the first Pentecost.

OTHER LITURGICAL DANCES

There are many other celebrations during the year that can call for a special use of dance. Two that have been exceptionally effective for me have been a baccalaureate and a wedding. In the baccalaureate liturgy at Boston College which takes place every year in a sports complex, the dance brings a visual beauty and focus to the celebration that it would lack without it. In alternative spaces for liturgy that are used for very large groups (convention center, stadium) the "secular" can be transformed into the "sacred" through movement and color that provides beauty and graciousness. In the Boston College baccalaureate, the most successful use of dance has been with Peloquin's *Lyric Liturgy* and his *Lord of Life.*

This particular wedding ritual had a special meaning since the bride and groom were both dancers and dance had become the way in which they expressed their faith. Their friends, other dancers, carried floral arches in procession that could be brought together to make a bridal arch, combined to form the symbol of the ring or simply make a beautiful visual pattern in the front of the space. After the exchange of vows, the dancers returned with the floral arches, dancing to Laetitia Blain's *Song of Meeting*, surrounding the newly married couple, finally creating a floral canopy over their heads. Since this was a special dance liturgy, in which the medium of dance was the primary mode of communication, there were many points in the liturgy that were danced. During the water rite the dancers passed flowers to all in the assembly. The responsorial psalm, Michael Joncas' *I Have Loved You,* was danced as was his *Praise His Name* for the Gospel acclamation. The bride and groom led the assembly in gesture prayer to a chanted *Our Father.* The communion meditation, *Be Not Afraid,* was danced as was the closing hymn, *Ode to Joy* (with special wedding lyrics). The entire ritual was a beautifully effective realization of the power of dance to communicate as a symbol in liturgy. Although it may seem to one who has only heard the ritual described, that there was "too much" dance, the experience of the people who were present was not that at all. Because of who the couple was, and given the integration of the dances into the flow of the ritual and the participation of the whole assembly in spirit and body, it was a ritual that communicated what it intended, namely, the love of two people as a sign of new life in the Church.

A renewed sense of the place of dance in liturgy is a sign of life for many in the Church. For others, it is a threatening manifestation of disintegration of standards and morals. Many will continue to fight vigorously against its inclusion as a valid means of religious expression in liturgical worship. If there is to be a meaningful dialogue between those who approve and those who disapprove, there must be an openness to learn from each other's perceptions and experiences, but in the last analysis people must be able to worship their God in ways that honestly express their faith. *Environment and Art in Catholic worship* says:

> Christians have not hesitated to use every human art in their celebration of the saving work of God in Jesus Christ, although in every historical period they have been influenced, at times inhibited, by cultural circumstances. In the resurrection of the Lord, all things are made new. Wholeness and healthiness are restored, because the reign of sin and death is conquered. Human limits are still real and we must be conscious of them. But we must also praise God and give God thanks with the human means we have available. God does not need liturgy; people do, and people have only their own arts and styles of expression with which to celebrate (4).

CHAPTER 4
Religious Dance in Performance

A second dimension of this dance exploration is the power of the dance to communicate religious experience in a "performance" situation. The principal reason for this interest is the artistic limitation put on strictly "liturgical dance" because of its integration into the larger context of the whole worship service. Ordinarily, a dance piece of more than five minutes in the liturgy would overpower and imbalance the rest of the ritual action. There are other avenues of exploration, however, for those who want to take the religious dynamics of human experience and express them through dance. In her book, *The Gospel According to Dance,* Giora Manor enumerates the ballet and modern dance works that have used bible stories as their inspiration. She says, "The rich dramatic biblical situations supply some choreographers with ready made scaffolds upon which to erect their dances. For others the Psalms or the book of Job are the means to convey philosophical thought in terms abstract, yet concrete enough to accommodate dance, the most physical of art forms, in which the sensual and spiritual meet."[5] She goes on to say, "An unparalleled tapestry of humanity is provided by the ancient anthology which is the Bible . . . it includes records of events which cast a shadow on the reputation of the sacred and revered personages, and celebrated heroes are presented with all their warts, making them human and very modern indeed."[6]

I have choreographed four major works based on biblical themes.

THE CHRISTMAS STORY

Music by Alan Hovhaness, Ralph Vaughan Williams
Choreographed by Rev. Robert VerEecke S.J.
Premiere—December 10, 1981

Prelude—"Ave Maria" from Triptych (Alan Hovhaness)
Nativity—"A Lark Ascending" (RVW)
Gloria in Excelsis—from Triptych
Good Tidings—Pastoral Symphony 3rd Movement (RVW)
Mary's Song and Pavane—"Job" (RVW)

This piece is the familiar story of Christmas in dance form. The first section emphasizes the human relationships in the story, specifically in the three characters, Mary, Joseph and Elizabeth. The second section is a dialogue between the angels and the shepherds. It is performed "en pointe" to create the ethereal "unearthly" quality of the vision of angels bringing "good tidings." The third section is a dialogue between the shepherds and the townspeople, who are resistant to believe the shepherds' story but who come to belief through the openness and wonder of their children. The final section is a reflective solo for Mary followed by a "pavane" of praise danced by the entire company.

TRILOGY

Music by Ralph Vaughan Williams
Choreographed by Rev. Robert VerEecke S.J.
Premiere—April 10, 1981

Birth—"A Lark Ascending"
Ministry—"Dives and Lazarus Variations"
Passion—Fantasia on a Theme of Thomas Tallis

This piece is choreographed in three parts. The first section is the same as the opening section of *The Christmas Story*. The second section begins with the encounter of the adult Jesus with John the Baptist. There are five short sections in this part that explore the dimensions of Jesus' relationships with different people: the disciples, Peter and John, Mary Magdalene, his mother, Mary, and others. This ministry section follows the basic dynamic of the gospel story: experiencing Jesus as a liberator, expecting him to be "Messiah" in a way that differs from his own sense of mission and a final reconciliation in the sharing of a meal. The third section is the Passion/Crucifixion as seen through the eyes of the two Marys, Mary Magdalene and Mary, the mother of Jesus. The piece ends with the traditional image of the "Pieta," mother holding her dead son in her arms. A recent addition to this piece is a short "resurrection" section as three women visit the tomb and find only the burial cloth. This is danced to a section of *Holy City* by Alan Hovhaness.

PROPHETS—THE CALL

Music by Olivier Messiaen (Quartet for the End of Time)
Choreographed by Rev. Robert VerEecke S.J.
Premiere—December 10, 1982

This piece is divided into three sections, one for each of the prophets: Isaiah, Jeremiah and Ezekiel. There is also a short concluding section. The focus of the piece is on the different calls each has received to be a "prophet." Isaiah's call happens in the context of a mystical vision of the throne of God. He is overwhelmed by his sense of unworthiness but responds to the call with the words, "Here I am. Send me." Jeremiah, on the other hand, is resistant to God's call. He wants no part of it, but ultimately cannot resist the force of that call. Ezekiel's call, like Isaiah's, is "mystical" but his is almost "psychedelic" in its details: the four beasts and the wheel. Ezekiel's acceptance of his call to be a prophet is symbolized by his "eating the scroll of the word of God." With each of the prophets is associated a major symbol that plays an important role in the prophet's word. For Isaiah, it is the "virgin who will conceive and bear a son." For Jeremiah, it is the people who are his antagonists, plotting his destruction for speaking God's words. For Ezekiel it is the dry bones that come to life.

In addition to the three prophets there is a chorus of six women who, like a traditional Greek chorus, function in many different roles; the cherubim and seraphim, the "people who walked in darkness," Jeremiah's antagonists, Ezekiel's beasts, the "dry bones" come to life.

EASTER CANTATA

Music by Alan Hovhaness (from Triptych)
Choreographed by Rev. Robert VerEecke S.J.
Premiere—April 10, 1983

This piece is in five sections, the first three associated with the Passion, the last two with the Resurrection. The difference in this piece and the preceding, however, is that the religious content does not come from the explicitly religious text. The words of the text that speak about the death and resurrection of Jesus are only a backdrop for the emotional struggle of one character. The woman in black is seated in a chair. She begins to dance, expressing a grief from deep within. Other dancers dressed in black leotards and tights are at times the inner thoughts and conflicting emotions within the woman, and at times other "people" who try to comfort her, support her in her grief. It is this danced expression of human compassion and solidarity that leads to the final two sections in which the woman appears in a white dress and the other dancers are now clearly "people" dressed in white to celebrate with her a new experience of life and hope. The style of the first three sections is modern while the style of the last two is more balletic.

There has been a gradual genesis in my works as a choreographer. The focus of the work tends to be less explicitly "religious" in terms of a narrative that is already given and is becoming more psycho-spiritual. The challenge for me is to let the story, the ideas, the emotions, emerge from the movement and not the other way around. Through the example and instruction of an excellent teacher and choreographer, Margot Parsons, by choreographing "religious dances for performance," I am finding ways to realize my vision of faith which can come to expression through the plastic arts, through the medium of the dance.

CHAPTER 5
A Dancing
People of God

A group of people of different ages and backgrounds gathers on a Friday evening at the Cenacle Retreat House in Brighton, Massachusetts. There is expectation, apprehension, and some confusion in their minds as to why they have come. In the first session as they introduce themselves, they tell why they have been drawn to this weekend. The reasons vary from, "I wanted to see what it was like," to, "I don't have any idea!" It is the beginning of a weekend of "Prayer, Presence and Worship through Movement and Dance," or as it is otherwise called, a "Dance Retreat."

During this weekend, this group of people, some with dance training, others with "two left feet," will be transformed into a model of the "Dancing Church."

I began these dance retreats six years ago to meet a need for people who wanted to learn to pray with their bodies. Instead of a silent retreat, a dance retreat would explore how people could pray through movement. Many had found in themselves a desire to express their faith experience, especially the affective dimension of this experience, in an embodied prayer. Those who had received "baptism in the spirit" felt "moved" to give praise to God with their whole self. The dance retreat would provide an extended period of time to explore these dynamics of the human spirit.

The methodology used in these weekends is to take a religious theme, such as reconciliation, celebration, or thanksgiving, and embody that experience through gesture and movement. The group would explore, for example, the gestures that would best realize the experience of mercy, forgiveness and healing. Many were surprised to find the range of gesture and movement broader than they expected. There was always more than one way of movement expression for a particular human dynamic. It was not necessary to limit movement prayer to the "classical" prayer gesture in the Christian tradition—the praying hands. In fact, many did not know that *the* classical "orans" position is open arms with palms facing up, from elbow to hand extended vertically.

The very first dance retreat was modeled on the Spiritual Exercises of Saint Ignatius and used the dynamic of God's self-revelation/individual self-awareness/praise for acceptance. These themes were enfleshed through the music of Ralph Vaughan Williams in the *Sanctus/benedictus, Kyrie* and *Gloria* of the *Mass in G Minor.* Although the weekend was successful, it became clear that there was too much content, spiritually and physically. In the short period of a weekend, it was not possible to reflect on or move through a whole conversion experience. For that reason, subsequent retreats became more focused; exploring reconciliation, healing, or thanksgiving— one dynamic of the Spirit.

The structure of the weekend is usually the same. Participants first need to be comfortable with their bodies. Through a series of move-

ments designed to relax and explore the range of the body's movement, people begin to realize the possibility of moving in different ways, in different planes, with different intensities. They begin to see how the extension of an arm or hand, the rotation of the body on its axis, fall and recovery, can be a means of expression. Music that is familiar from a liturgical context is used for these beginning exercises, so that people associate the movements with the prayer/worship context in which they are used to hearing it. (*Lord of Light* by the St. Louis Jesuits has an excellent variety in tempo, feeling and rhythm.) Following these initial exercises, the whole group works on an entrance procession, choreographed by the director of the retreat. Through mutual support, the participants learn from each other. Those with training assist those who are uncomfortable or insecure. At the end of the first night, it seems impossible that these "steps" can become a community's prayer. For the next two days, participants actively engage in learning dances and exploring their personal creative prayer. Using musical settings of the psalms, small groups work together to find visual images, movement themes, and gestures that capture for them the inner dynamic of the psalm. Certain basic movement principles are given to aid the process: don't make literal interpretations, try to find a sustaining emotion that can be communicated in one or two thematic movements on which one can build and develop, concentrate on the movement flow so that transitions are clearly seen. The results of these movement-prayer improvisations have varied from "good try" to "excellent." At the end of the weekend, there is a remarkable sense of unity that comes from the experience of sharing and working together through movement. The final liturgy in which all of the dances are brought together has been a consistently beautiful realization of the dream and vision of a dancing church.

The following are some of the themes that have been used for the dance retreats:

— Divine grace through human graciousness: the body in prayer.

— Eucharist: how and why do we give thanks

— The inner dynamics of celebration: gathering, listening, responding

— Reconciliation: called to a new experience of God and ourselves

— Easter: celebration of new life

— Community: building the City of God together

— Lent: a time to be re-created

— Eucharist: the way we remember

— Easter joy: do we really have reason to rejoice?

The following are some of the musical selections that have been used

with the preceding themes:

		Taken From
St. Louis Jesuits:	Be Not Afraid	
	Glory and Praise	
	You Are Near	
	Come to the Water	
	Redeemer Lord	
	Jesus the Lord	
	City of God	
	This Alone	
	Sing a New Song	
	Here I Am Lord	
	I Lift Up My Soul	
Michael Joncas:	On Eagle's Wings	
	Praise His Name	
	As the Watchman	
	I Have Loved You	
Lucien Deiss:	As the Young Seek to be Fed	
	In Those Days	
Carey Landry:	Jesus Is Life	
Pachelbel:	Canon in D	
Stephen Schwartz:	All Good Gifts	
C. Alexander Peloquin:	Out of the Depths	*An American Liturgy*
	His Love Is Everlasting	*Songs of Israel I*
	This Is the Day	"
	Taste and See	"
	Lord, Send Out Your Spirit	"
	My God, My God	"
	Shout for Joy	"
	Let Us Go Rejoicing	*Songs of Israel II*
	Lord Jesus, Come	*Lyric Liturgy*
	Alleluia	"
	Gloria	"
	Ave, Ave	*Unless You Become*
	Praise to the Lord	*Lord of Life*
	Alleluia	"
	Now Thank We All our God	"

Conclusions

In conclusion, a personal note and a contemporary setting of an ancient psalm:

I believe in a dancing God who has gifted his people with the ability to express their joy, their pain, their hopes and visions through gesture, movement and dance. I believe in a "people of God" who are invited to respond to God's love with their whole being, mind, body and spirit and I pray with that "dancing people of God" this ancient prayer:

PSALM 150

TO YOU
to you above
to you above holy
and strong,
be joy
be joy from us
for boundless lifegiving
power,
joy from
our trumpets, joy
from our lyrical strings,
joy from
our drums
and dances and
harps, pipes and shivering
cymbals,
joy from
our clashing, our
ringing with all that lives
to You![7]

Notes

[1]Gerard Manley Hopkins, *The Poems of Gerard Manley Hopkins*, ed. W.H. Gardner and N.H. Mackenzie (London: Oxford University Press, 1967), p. 66.

[2]"Dance in Liturgy," *The Canon Law Digest* VIII, pp. 78-82.

[3]Lawrence J. Johnson, *The Mystery of Faith: The Ministers of Music* (Washington, D.C.: National Association of Pastoral Musicians, 1983), p. 87.

[4]Jean LaPlace, *Prayer According to the Scriptures*, translated and edited by M.L. Powell, r.c. (Brighton, MA: Religious of the Cenacle, 1978), p. 3.

[5]Giora Manor, *The Gospel According the Dance* (New York: Saint Martin's Press, 1980), p. 23.

[6]*Ibid.*, p. 24.

[7]Francis Sullivan, *Lyric Psalms: Half a Psalter* (Washington, D.C.: National Association of Pastoral Musicians, 1983), p. 24.

DOCUMENT SOURCES

Constitution on the Sacred Liturgy (Sacrosanctum Concilium), The Documents of Vatican II, 1963.

Directory for Masses with Children, Bishops' Committee on the Liturgy, (Washington, D.C.: United States Catholic Conference, 1973).

Environment and Art in Catholic Worship, Bishops' Committee on the Liturgy, (Washington, D.C.: United States Catholic Conference, 1978).

Annotated Bibliography

by Gloria Weyman

Adams, Doug. *Congregational Dancing in Christian Worship.* 2d rev. ed., North Aurora, Illinois: The Sharing Co., 1980.
.... *Involving the People in Dancing Worship: Historic & Contemporary Patterns.* North Aurora, Illinois: The Sharing Co., 1975.
Alberts, David. *Pantomine: Elements and Exercises.* Lawrence, Kansas: University Press of Kansas, 1971.
Amberg, George. *Art in Modern Ballet.* New York: Pantheon Books, 1946.
Andrews, Edward D. *The Gift to Be Simple: Songs, Dances, and Rituals of the American Shakers.* Locust Valley, New York: J.J. Augustin, Publisher, 1940. Republished New York: Dover Publications, 1962.
Armitage, Merle. *Dance Memoranda.* New York: Duell, Sloan & Pierce, 1947.
Arvey, Verna. *Choreographic Music: Music for the Dance.* New York: E. P. Dutton & Co., 1941.

Backman, E. Louis. *Religious Dances in the Christian Church and in Popular Medicine.* Translated by E. Classen. London: Allen & Unwin, 1952.
Backman presents the appearance and significance of religious dances in the Church and Christian society from the beginnings of Christianity until today. He tries to discover the historically determined significance, the earliest explanation and the motivation behind various symbols and rituals.
Barlin, Anne and Paul. *The Art of Learning Through Movement.* This is a nicely illustrated manual for those who need help in the areas of movement and creativity. Two records provide accompaniment.
Barlin, Anne Lief and Greenberg, Tamara Robbin. *Move and Be Moved: A Practical Approach to Movement with Meaning.* This book provides practical exercises for body awareness and dance/movement response for high school, college and adult levels.
Berk, Fred. *The Jewish Dance.* New York: Exposition Press, 1960.
Best, David. *Expression in Movement and the Arts: A Philosophical Inquiry.* Boston: Plays, Inc., 1980.
Bibliographic Guide to Dance: 1982. Boston: G. K. Hall & Co., 1983.
This is a comprehensive reference collection of material relating to all aspects of dance—from theatrical to religious—and to every type of dance—from ballet to folk.
Blom, Lynne Anne and Chaplin, L. Tarin. *The Intimate Act of Choreography.* Pittsburgh: University of Pittsburgh Press, 1982.

The authors cover everything from the basics of time, space, and form to the more sophisticated areas of abstraction and choreographic devices.

Bruce, Violet R. and Tooke, Joan D. *Lord of the Dance: An Approach to Religious Education.* New York: Pergamon Press, 1966.

C

Cheney, Gay and Strader, Janet. *The Modern Dance.* Boston: Allyn and Bacon, Inc.
Philosophy and practicality are combined in this beautifully written approach to choreography and technique. The chapters include helpful "Learning Experiences."

Clark, James M. *The Dance of Death: In the Middle Ages and the Renaissance.* Glasgow: Jackson, Son & Co., 1950.

Clarke, Mary and Crisp, Clement. *A History of Dance.* New York: Crown Publishers, Inc., 1981.
This richly illustrated volume shows the important role that dance has played for over 2,000 years. Although emphasizing classical ballet and modern Western dance, it touches on every major form of dance in the world.

Cox, Harvey. *The Feast of Fools: A Theological Essay on Festivity and Fantasy.* Cambridge: Harvard University Press, 1969.

D

Daniels, Marilyn. *The Dance in Christianity: A History of Religious Dance Through the Ages.* New York: Paulist Press, 1981.
Daniels traces the role of dance in Christianity from biblical times to the present and explores the important place dance had in liturgical ceremonies of the first five centuries.

Davies, J. G. *Worship and Dance.* Birmingham, Alabama: University of Birmingham, 1975.

Deiss, Lucien and Weyman, Gloria Gabriel. *Dancing for God.* Chicago: World Library of Sacred Music, 1965.

.... *Dance for the Lord.* Chicago: World Library Publications, Inc., 1975.
This book presents precedents from the Bible and early Church history for religious dance, along with practical suggestions and choreography for eleven liturgical dances.

.... *Dance as Prayer.* Chicago: World Library Publications, Inc., 1979.
Excerpted and revised from *Dance for the Lord,* this booklet is a guide for better, more reverent and dignified dancing in today's liturgy.

.... *Louez Dieu par la Danse.* Paris: Les Editions du Levain, 1981.

.... *Liturgical Dance.* Phoenix, Arizona: North American Liturgy Resources, 1984.

This book explains why, according to the Scripture, ordinary parish communities should dance for the Lord. Practical suggestions, detailed choreography for nine songs, and a music cassette are provided. (These dances are also available on video cassette.)

DeMille, Agnes. *The Book of Dance.* London: Paul Hamlyn Ltd., 1963.
The historical and artistic development of dance is presented with beautiful illustrations.

Denby, Edwin. *Looking at the Dance.* New York: Pellegrini & Cudahy, 1949.

DeSola, Carla. *Learning Through Movement.* New York: Paulist Press, 1974.
This book teaches how to use dance as an exercise for self-discovery.

.... *The Spirit Moves: A Handbook of Dance and Prayer.* Washington, D.C.: The Liturgical Conference, 1977.

Dietering, Carolyn. *Actions, Gestures, and Bodily Attitudes.* Saratoga, California: Resource Publications, Inc., 1980.

Duffy Natalie Willman. *Modern Dance: An Adult Beginner's Guide.* Englewood Cliffs, N.J.: Prentice-Hall, Inc., 1982.
Illustrations, theories, techniques, choreography, and appendices make this a valuable guide for the beginning student and the teacher.

Duncan, Isadora. *Art of the Dance.* New York: Theatre Arts. 1928.

E

Eliade, Mircea. *The Sacred and the Profane.* New York: Harper & Row, 1961.

Ellfeldt, Lois. *A Primer for Choreographers.* Palo Alto, California: Mayfield Publishing Co., 1967.
Beginners will find suggestions and insights into the process of choreography.

Ellfeldt, Lois and Carne, Edwin. *Dance Productions Handbook or Later Is Too Late.* Palo Alto, California: Mayfield Publishing Co.
Here are helpful suggestions for costumes, lighting, and staging for liturgical dance or church pageants.

Ellis, Havelock. *The Dance of Life.* Boston: Houghton Mifflin Co., 1923.

F

Feldenkais, Moshe. *Awareness Through Movement.* New York: Harper & Row, 1973.
The author gives practical health exercises for personal growth and the development of a good self-image.

Fischer, Balthasuar. *Signs, Words & Gestures: Short Homilies on the Liturgy.* Translated by Matthew J. O'Connell. New York: Pueblo Publishing Co., 1981.

Foatelli, Renee. *Les Danses Religieuses dans le Christianisme.* Paris: Editions Spes, 1947.

Fraser, Sir John. *The Golden Bough.* New York: The Macmillan Company, 1947.
The author explores the beginnings of dance and celebration in legends, myths, customs and traditions.

Frazer, Louise. *Ballet: The Art Defined.*
This book for beginners and professional dancers defines technical terms for positions, techniques, and directions used in classical ballet. It also provides beneficial stretching exercises.

G

Gopal, Ram. *Indian Dancing.* London: Phoenix House, 1951.

Gross, J. B. *The Parson on Dancing.* Brooklyn, New York: Dance Horizons, 1977.
The author discusses dancing as it is taught in the Bible and was practiced among the ancient Greeks and Romans.

Gunther, Bernard and Fusco, Paul. *Sense Relaxation: Below Your Mind.* New York: Collier Books, 1968.
This book shows how to tone the body and ease tension through simple sensory exercises.

H

Hanna, Judith Lynne. *To Dance Is Human: A Theory of Nonverbal Communication.* Austin, Texas: University of Texas Press, 1979.

Haskell, Arnold L. *The Wonderful World of Dance.* Garden City, New York: Garden City Books, 1960.
The author gives a good historical background of dance.

Highwater, Jamake. *Dance: Rituals of Experience.* New York: A and W Publishing Co., 1978.

Humphrey, Doris. *The Art of Making Dances.* Edited by Barbara Pollack. New York: Holt, Rinehart and Winston, 1962.
This book gives very helpful guidelines for choreography.

K

Keen, Sam. *To a Dancing God.* New York: Harper & Row, 1970.

Kinney, Troy and Margaret. *The Dance: Its Place in Art and Life.* rev. ed. Frederick A. Stokes Co., 1914.

Kipnis, Claude. *The Mime Book.* New York: Harper & Row, 1974.
The author uses excellent photographs to clearly explain the techniques and theory of mime in a fascinating way.

Kirk, Martha Ann. *Dancing With Creation.* Saratoga, California: Resource Publications, Inc., 1983.

Kirstein, Lincoln. *Dance: A Short History of Classic Theatrical Dancing.* Brooklyn, New York: Dance Horizons, 1969.

Koegler, Horst. *The Concise Oxford Dictionary of Ballet.* 2d.ed. New York: Oxford University Press, Inc., 1982.
This comprehensive reference book covers 400 years of dance.

Kriegsman, Sali Ann. *Modern Dance in America: The Bennington Years.* Boston: G. K. Hall & Co., 1981.
This is an outstanding documentary of the development of modern dance from 1934-1942.

L

Lawson, Joan. *Mime: The Theory and Practice of Expressive Gesture.* Brooklyn, N.Y.: Dance Horizons.
Lenvel, Helene Lubienska de. *The Whole Man at Worship: The Actions of Man before God.* Translated by Rachel Attwater. New York: Desclee Co., 1961.
Letherman, Leroy. *Martha Graham: Portrait of the Lady as an Artist.* New York: Knopf, 1966.
The author gives an inside look at how the intuition of this outstanding woman enhanced her creativity.

M

Marks, Josheph E. *America Learns to Dance.* Brooklyn, New York: Dance Horizons, 1976.
This is a historical study of dance education in America before 1900.
Martin, John. *America Dancing: The Background and Personalities of the Modern Dance.* New York: Dodge, 1936.
May, Rollo, ed. *Symbolism in Religion and Literature.* New York: Braziller, 1960.
Mead, G. R. S. *The Sacred Dance in Christendom.* "Quest Reprint Series," No. 2. London: John M. Watkins, 1926.
Mettler, Barbara. *Materials of Dance as a Creative Art Activity.* Tuscon, Arizona: Mettler Studios, 1960.
To make creative dance easy and enjoyable for any age group, this book gives many ideas and exercises for several lessons in various areas of dance, keeping in mind a progression of development.
Money, Keith. *Anna Pavlova: Her life and Art.* New York: Knopf, 1982.
Mynatt, Constance V. and Kaiman, Bernard D. *Folk Dancing for Students and Teachers.* Dubuque, Iowa: Wm. C. Brown Publishers, 1968.

N

Nadel, Myron H. and Miller, Constance, eds. *The Dance Experience: Readings in Dance Appreciation.* Englewood, New Jersey: Universe Publishing Co., 1978.
This book discusses topics such as the nature of dance, forms of dance, problems in dance and facets of dance education.

O

Oesterly, W.O.E. *The Sacred Dance: A Study in Comparative Folklore.* New York: Macmillan, 1923.
Ortegel, Sr. Adelaide, S.P. *A Dancing People.* West Lafayette, Indiana: The Center for Contemporary Celebration, 1976.

Ortegel, Sr. Adelaide, S.P. and Schneider, Rev. Kent E. *Light: A Language of Celebration.* West Lafayette, Indiana: The Center for Contemporary Celebration, 1973.
This book gives techniques on how to use projected light creatively to add another dimension to movement improvisations.

Phenix, Philip H. *Education and the Worship of God.* Philadelphia: The Westminster Press, 1966.
The chapter on "Art as the Work of God" explores the relationship of art and theology.

Pieper, Josef. *In Tune with the World: A Theory of Festivity.* New York: Harcourt, Brace and World, 1963.

R

Rahner, Hugo. *Man at Play.* Translated by Brian Battershaw and Edward Quinn. New York: Herder and Herder, 1972.

Ritter, Richard H. *The Arts of the Church.* Boston: Pilgrim Press, 1947.

Rivers, Clarence Jos. *Soulful Worship.* Washington, D.C.: Office for Black Catholics, 1974.

Rogers, Frederick R., ed. *Dance: A Basic Educational Technique.* New York: Macmillan, 1941.

S

Sacks, Curt. *The World History of Dance.* New York: W. W. Norton & Co., 1957.

St. Denis, Ruth. *An Unfinished Life: An Autobiography.* New York: Harper & Bros., 1939.

Schneider, Rev. Kent E. *The Creative Musician in the Church.* West Lafayette, Indiana: The Center for Contemporary Celebration, 1976.

Schneider, Rev. Kent E. ed. *Directory of Artists and Religious Communities.* West Lafayette, Indiana: The Center for Contemporary Celebration, 1975.

Seldon, Elizabeth. *The Dancer's Quest: Essays on the Aesthetic of the Contemporary Dance.* Berkeley, California: University of California Press, 1935.

Shawn, Ted. *Every Little Movement.* New York: Ted Shawn, 1954.

Shelton, Suzanne. *Divine Dancer: A Biography of Ruth St. Denis.* New York: Doubleday & Co., Inc., 1981.

Sherbon, Elizabeth. *On the Count of One: A Guide to Movement and Progression in Dance.* Palo Alto, California: National Press Books.

Shreeves, Rosamund. *Movement and Educational Dance for Children.* Boston: Plays, Inc., 1980.
This practical guide describes activities, relates dance and movement to various stimuli, and provides tested lessons.

Sorell, Walter. *The Dance Through the Ages.* New York: Grosset & Dunlap, 1967.
The author traces the history of dance from primitive rites and tribal dances to modern day dancers who are expanding the field.

Stegemeir, Henri. *The Dance of Death in Folksong, with an Introduction on the History of the Dance of Death.* Chicago: University of Chicago Libraries, 1939.

Strong, Roy, Guest, Ivor and Buckle, Richard. *Designing for the Dancer.* Englewood, N.J.: Universe Publishing Co., 1982.
For everyone interested in costume design, this is an illustrated history of dance costumes by famous experts and designers from the 15th to the 20th century.

Taylor, Margaret Fisk. *A Time for Dance: Symbolic Movement in Worship.* Revised and reprinted Doug Adams, ed. North Aurora, Illinois: The Sharing Co., 1976.

Terry, Walter. *The Dance in America.* New York: Harper & Row, 1956.

Turner, Margery J. *New Dance: Approaches to Non-literal Choreography.* Pittsburgh: University of Pittsburgh Press, 1976.
This approach to non-literal dance, which includes chapters on music and dance, and lighting and dance, gives specific assignments to sharpen the skills of all choreographers.

Urlin, Ethel. *Dancing, Ancient and Modern.* New York: Appleton & Co., 1914.

Vuiller, Gaston. *The History of Dancing.* New York: Appleton & Co., 1898.

Warren, Florence. *The Dance of Death.* Oxford University Press, 1931.

Wiener, Jack and Lidstone, John. *Creative Movement for Children: A Dance Program for the Classroom.* New York: Van Nostrand Reinhold Company, 1969.
A practical explanation of a challenging program. The book uses beautiful photographs of children in creative movement.

Wosien, Maria-Gabriele. *Sacred Dance-Encounter with the Gods.* London: Avon Books, 1974.
This beautifully illustrated book traces humanity's spiritual journey in the religions of the world as expressed through sacred dance.